Grit & Grace
A Women Writing Anthology

DeVonna R. Allison, Monica Clark, Hedy Habra,
Ingrid Lochamire, Kathleen McGookey, Adela Najarro,
Traci Rhoades, Patricia Jabbeh Wesley

Managing Editor:
Shanda Blue Easterday, Faun River Press

Author/Editors: DeVonna Allison,
Monica Clark and Ingrid Lochamire

Suite 300 - 990 Fort St
Victoria, BC, V8V 3K2
Canada

www.friesenpress.com

Copyright © 2018 by Shanda Blue Easterday
First Edition — 2018

All rights reserved.

No part of this publication may be reproduced in any form, or by any means, electronic or mechanical, including photocopying, recording, or any information browsing, storage, or retrieval system, without permission in writing from FriesenPress.

ISBN
978-1-5255-2987-0 (Hardcover)
978-1-5255-2988-7 (Paperback)
978-1-5255-2989-4 (eBook)

1. LITERARY COLLECTIONS

Distributed to the trade by The Ingram Book Company

Table of Contents

Fiction

On the Nights Tooley Plays
Monica Clark
3

My Brother, Ambrose
Monica Clark
8

Tyler at Camp Amigo
Monica Clark
19

Morning on the River
Monica Clark
32

You Make Your Choices
Monica Clark
36

Poetry

Beth Anne
DeVonna Allison
53

That Night upon the Moors
Monica Clark
54

Walking at Dawn on a Foggy Day
Monica Clark
55

Whose Woods?
Monica Clark
56

Time, Like Frost
Monica Clark
57

Garden Toad
Monica Clark
58

Hummingbird
Monica Clark
59

Poker Troubles
Monica Clark
60

Night Visitor
Monica Clark
62

Abstract
Shanda Blue Easterday
63

Chloasma
Shanda Blue Easterday
64

Cleave
Shanda Blue Easterday
65

Feet
Shanda Blue Easterday
66

Cucurbita pepo
Shanda Blue Easterday
67

Floor
Shanda Blue Easterday
68

Leash Slipped
Shanda Blue Easterday
69

Matter
Shanda Blue Easterday
70

Trying Not to Think
Shanda Blue Easterday
71

Reading by Candlelight
Hedy Habra
72

After the Storm
Hedy Habra
73

Tea at *Chez Paul's*
Hedy Habra
75

Blue Heron
Hedy Habra
78

Open-Air Cinema
in Heliopolis
Hedy Habra
80

A Pantoum in Flight
Ingrid Lochamire
82

Fairy Tale
Kathleen McGookey
83

Pain Lake
Kathleen McGookey
84

Lighthouse Tour, South
Manitou Island
Kathleen McGookey
85

Red Ants, Black Ants
Adella Najaro
86

Cleaning House
Adela Najarro
88

Near Traverse City, Michigan
Adela Najarro
90

The Swarming Background
Adela Najarro
91

San Francisco
Adela Najarro
93

Lauds
Donna Perkins Pierce
95

My Teacher
Donna Perkins Pierce
96

November Garden
Donna Perkins Pierce
98

Too Many Chickens Are
Coming Home to Roost
Patricia Jabbeh Wesley
99

Suburbia
Patricia Jabbeh Wesley
101

In Case of Water Landing
Patricia Jabbeh Wesley
103

Shakespeare 550
Patricia Jabbeh Wesley
106

Poem Written from Failed Chat Notes
Patricia Jabbeh Wesley
109

Creative Non-Fiction

Of Sukkah and Muezzins
DeVonna R. Allison
115

Encounter
DeVonna R. Allison
118

Field of Geese
DeVonna R. Allison
120

Flight 93
DeVonna R. Allison
123

Locked Out
DeVonna R. Allison
127

Sans Air
DeVonna R. Allison
131

Grandma's Baby
DeVonna R. Allison
135

On the Train from Milan
Monica Clark
138

Rabbits, Rats and Pineapples
Monica Clark
141

Groundhog Days
Monica Clark
144

Shards
Monica Clark
146

The Holiness of Diversity
Ingrid Lochamire
149

The Way It Is with Children
Ingrid Lochamire
155

Coffee Break
Ingrid Lochamire
159

The Work of Grandma's Hands
Traci Rhoades
161

Memoir

Like a Phoenix
Ingrid Lochamire
169

Black Birds
Ingrid Lochamire
174

A Season of Miracles
Ingrid Lochamire
176

Nashville
Ingrid Lochamire
178

Redeeming Mother's Day
Ingrid Lochamire
181

Ashes
Ingrid Lochamire
190

A Walk Among the Tombstones
Ingrid Lochamire
193

"Assisted Living"
Ingrid Lochamire
196

Stones
Ingrid Lochamire
198

An Unexpected Journey
Ingrid Lochamire
200

Author Biographies
211

Art Credits
217

Fiction

On the Nights Tooley Plays
Monica Clark

On the nights Tooley plays, Beau and I race up to the roof as soon as the sun sets. Big trucks groan and rumble and sirens whine on the street below us. Tiny cars scoot around like toys. On the roof, Beau and I are giants.

Daddy brings the chairs and a bucket filled with ice and soda, and Momma lights a candle in the middle of the little table. The tang of citronella rises as the flame flickers and dances with the dark.

Tooley nights are special. Even the pale, weary moon grinning down at us knows that. Footsteps sound on the steps as other neighbors join us. They bring lawn chairs and laughter with them. Finally, Tooley, slow and steady, climbs the stairs. Beau and I race to help him, and he leans on my shoulder while Beau takes the battered case from Tooley's gnarled hand. With a groan, Tooley eases himself into a chair and Momma pours him a glass of tea from the pitcher on the table.

"Miz Johnson, your sweet tea surely is a taste of home," says Tooley, taking the tall glass from Momma's hand.

"I'm glad you like it, Mr. Tooley," says Momma, and she blushes just a little. "I thank you for teaching me to make it. New Orleans must be a wonderful place," she says gently.

"Yes, ma'am, it is," Tooley says. "And I'm a New Orleans man, born and bred."

On the roof, the cinders are still warm under our feet. On hot days, the tar melts into gummy goo, and the sharp twang of asphalt fills our noses. A few weak stars wink in the night sky, but the lights from the city masks most of them. Thankfully, the traffic sounds are muted this far above the street. I look around at friends and neighbors, people we have lived beside for years, but did not know until after Tooley came to live with us.

Tooley smiles as he opens his trumpet case. He looks at the trumpet and gently strokes the rim of the horn with the tips of his fingers before lifting it out of the battered little box. Reverently, he lifts the horn and fits it to his lips. Music rings out over the city as Tooley starts to play. Windows open and folks lean out, trying to catch the sound of Tooley's horn. Tooley seems young and strong again. His music is a miracle.

I close my eyes and let the notes carry me to places I have never seen; to a wide and lazy river flowing out to the sea along crowded, narrow streets filled with people laughing and dancing, across misty marshes and moon-spattered beaches to the docks where the boats rise and fall, cradled in star-struck silver waves.

Daddy's grand-uncle Tooley came to live with us after Hurricane Katrina destroyed his home. The storm changed many lives, and not for the better.

"Sadie," Momma told me, "you are going to have to give up your room. You can bunk with Beau while Mr. Tooley is with us."

"What?" I said, and then I uttered what children have proclaimed throughout history, "But, Momma, that's not fair!"

"Sadie Elizabeth!" Momma scolded me. "Fair? Do you think it was fair for Mr. Tooley to nearly drown in the only home he has ever known? Do you think it is fair that he lost everything?"

I looked down, shame-faced, and in the end, I had to give up my big, four-poster bed and the matching white dresser. I had to give up my bookshelves and my stuffed animals. Worst of all, I had to give up my privacy and share a room with my stinky younger brother who talked endlessly, even in his sleep. So that summer I, too, learned a few things about losing everything.

The dour old man who arrived on our doorstep, downtrodden and slump-shouldered, carried only a small cardboard box filled with all his worldly possessions. He hardly spoke to us and spent the whole first month shut up in his room.

"Leave him be," Momma warned us, and Beau and I were quiet as mice those first few weeks. It was tiring, Momma hushing us anytime we made a noise.

Beau and I took turns setting a tray of food in front of Tooley's door, and many times the tray sat there until morning.

Then one day Momma took Tooley out for an appointment.

"You children behave while I'm gone," Momma said, giving us a look.

Beau and I, looking properly chastened, nodded, assuring Momma that we would be angels while she was gone. But as soon as the front door hit the frame, Beau and I headed to Tooley's room—to my room.

We were curious about the old man who meant nothing to us then. All we knew was he had almost died in New Orleans, he was sad, and he was our problem now.

"Look, he doesn't even make his bed." Beau pointed to the rumpled sheets. "And eww, what's that smell?"

A sharp, menthol smell filled the room, and a tub of liniment sat next to the bed. A dab of yellow goo ran down its side and a glob of it rested on the wood of my nightstand. I was outraged.

"He's ruining everything!" I told Beau.

"What's this?" Beau asked, holding a small, beat-up suitcase that neither of us had seen before.

"I don't know." I shrugged. "Open it and find out."

Beau sat the case on the bed and undid the latch. Slowly, he pushed up the lid. Despite its age, the horn glistened in the light, set deep in the worn, velvet form of the case. It lay there begging me to pick it up. My fingers trembled. Did I dare?

I found myself reaching for it, and as I brought the thing to my lips I heard Momma's voice.

"Sadie Elizabeth Johnson! What in heaven's name do you think you are doing?" Momma's voice was hot with anger. She stood in the doorway, hands on her hips, glaring down at me and at Beau.

Tooley stood slightly behind her and for the first time I saw something in his eyes besides the sadness that he usually wore like an old coat. He looked at me curiously and cocked his head.

I tried to explain. "But Momma, we just, I just..."

"Out! Both of you! Out, now!" Momma pointed to the hall.

"I'm sorry, Momma. Sorry, Mr. Tooley," I stammered. "I didn't mean to..." but Momma's glare dried up all my words and I set the golden horn back in the box and closed the latch.

"Out!" Momma ordered, and Beau and I ran out of the room as if we were on fire.

That night, Momma had a long talk with us about respect and privacy and sent us to our room without supper. It was late spring, but the room was hot and stuffy. I lay there sweating and feeling sorry for myself.

"It's not fair," I thought, and then I heard it. Through the wall came faint notes of music. I thought I was dreaming at first, but then the notes grew strong and loud. Just for a moment, Tooley played his trumpet. I listened for it again late into the night, but if Tooley played, I never heard it. That night, music chased and filled my dreams.

Tooley joined us for breakfast the next morning, and every morning after that. Something healed in the broken old man. Soon, Tooley's deep laughter filled our apartment.

One night, Tooley found his way up to the roof. He practiced there, and one Saturday night he played a concert.

I think of those long summer nights; they were some of the best nights of my life. Tooley's music was bittersweet. The blues sailed out of his trumpet, sad and lonely as the whistle of a far-off train. Jazz streamed out, bright as polished brass, shiny as a new penny. Tooley's music flew with wings across the night sky.

Some nights, Tooley played until a glimmer of light opened the eastern sky. Often Beau would fall asleep, head resting on a table. But I would stay awake. I didn't want to miss a note of Tooley's music.

On my eleventh birthday, Tooley found a used trumpet in a pawn store and taught me to play it. Those sultry nights on top of our old apartment building on Turner Street still fill my dreams. Perhaps that is what drove me to New Orleans.

Today, I am twenty-one, and clutched in my hand is Tooley's old trumpet case. I breathe the salt air and hear the squawk of seagulls along the harbor. I wind my way through the throngs of people along Bourbon Street until I find the little club where Tooley played until a hurricane changed his life, changed all our lives.

My fingers drum nervously on the scarred black case, but I know I have been taught by the best. My music was molded by a master musician. I play for myself tonight, and I play for Tooley. It is the least I can do to thank him for all the nights Tooley played.

My Brother, Ambrose
Monica Clark

Ambrose stopped that night in the cold November fog long enough to chuck a rock at the lame cat standing ghostlike alongside the road. Thin and mangy, the cat had been skulking around our neighborhood for the last few months. One night I saw it perched on the roof outside my bedroom window, yellow eyes gleaming in the moonlight. I felt sorry for the poor thing, starving and homeless, missing a front paw, but I already had enough to worry about. I didn't have time to think about a stray animal.

Ambrose hated the cat. He always chased after it and sometimes he threw rocks at it, usually missing, but not tonight. Tonight, the pitiful creature let out a startled, wrenching yowl and limped away, disappearing into the shadows.

"Don't do that, Ambrose," I said quietly. "He's got it tough enough already."

Ambrose glared at me, and I flinched, then he shrugged and started down the road again. I wanted to say more, but if I did, Ambrose might just start chucking rocks at me, so I stopped. I watched my brother limp down the road until he, too, disappeared in the gloom. A part of me wished he'd disappear forever.

No, I don't hate Ambrose, if that's what you're thinking. It'd be easier if I did. It's just that I remember the way he used to be. Before the accident. Before the funeral. Before Daddy started drinking. I remember when everybody loved Ambrose.

He was the best at anything he set out to do. By the time he was twelve, my brother, Ambrose, was the strongest athlete at our school. He could outrun the older boys, and he was an artist with a baseball bat in his hands. He'd whack a ball anywhere he wanted, no matter what was pitched at him.

The afternoon everything changed, Ambrose was teaching me to bat. I was using a rough pine bat he had made me. He had shaved off all the bark and my hands were sticky with pine sap; the sharp smell of it made my nose tingle.

"Relax, Tom, don't clutch it so tight." He laughed.

I stood there, hot and sweaty, trying to hold up the makeshift bat.

"Okay, here it comes."

He lobbed an easy pitch to me, and I swung. I didn't hit the ball head on, but I nicked it and it flew across the yard, bounced a few times, and landed near Mama's garden.

"Great, Tom! You're getting the hang of it. When we get a proper bat, there'll be no stopping you!"

A warm feeling rose in me, and I knew, *I knew*, he was right. Ambrose had a way of making me feel like I could do anything. And it wasn't just me. Everyone wanted to be around Ambrose then. Everyone wanted to be his friend.

Once, there was this new kid at school. I can't think of his name. He wasn't there very long, but you could tell he was a sad case. His family was renting the old Wilson place out at the end of Cabbage Road. The Wilson house was hardly holding itself upright. It slanted and leaned and shivered when the wind blew. There was no running water, no inside toilet. Even the outhouse stood crooked in the yard.

The kid who showed up at school the first day of September looked to be in about the same, sad, sorry shape as that old house. He was dirty and he smelled bad. His clothes were old and used thin. His shirt was way too tight, and the kid's pants were high above his boney ankles. There were holes at the knees, except now the holes were up to the kid's thighs, and white patches of skin poked through the frayed cotton. Even his shoes were a mess. One of them flapped when he walked.

Right away, everyone started making fun of him. I can still see him walking down the road that first day, his head hung low, trying not to cry.

The next day, it started all over again. The kid slunk up the school steps wearing the same beat-up, dirty clothes he'd worn the day before.

"Hey, Flapper, get some new shoes, will ya?" one of the older boys yelled.

We all watched to see what the kid would do, but the kid knew he was beat. His shoulders slumped, and his eyes were stuck to the ground.

Then my brother, Ambrose, walked down the steps. He stuck out his hand and said, "Hi, I'm Ambrose."

The new kid flinched like Ambrose was going to punch him. He stood there, wide-eyed and frightened, like a doe I surprised once in the woods, all panicky and ready to run. I guess he thought it was a joke or something. It got quiet then, like church when the preacher clears his throat just before he starts up. The kid's face turned bright red.

"Come with me," Ambrose said. "I have an idea."

Ambrose led him into school, past all the other boys, his arm around the kid's shoulder.

The next time we saw him, the kid's shoe wasn't flapping anymore. There was a big wad of tape wrapped around it. Ambrose ate lunch with the new boy and played catch with him at recess, too.

When school was out, the kid followed us home like a lost puppy. But he wasn't lost, Ambrose invited him. Michael was his name. Anyway, Ambrose took Michael into the shed and found some tiny nails Daddy kept out there. He fixed Michael's shoe for good, and Ambrose talked Mama into giving Michael some of his old clothes.

"Mama, I don't ever wear this," Ambrose said, holding up his best Sunday shirt, daring Mama to correct him. "We should let Michael have it." He grinned.

What could Mama say? She smiled a tight little smile, then she got a good eyeful of Michael, and she and Ambrose managed to find a couple pairs of pants and a good coat that would've been mine that next fall when Ambrose outgrew it. There was even a pair of Ambrose's old shoes. They were worn, but still better than what Michael had on his feet.

Michael hung his head. "Ma'am, I can't take no charity. My pa'll skin me if I take them things home. I appreciate y'all thinkin' of me, but..."

"Nonsense," Mama told him.

Somehow, the two of them, Mama and Ambrose, convinced Michael he would be doing them a big favor taking those clothes. You could see the yearning and the hope swelling in the boy's eyes.

"I don't think my pa..." he stammered, but Mama wasn't listening.

"Come on, boys, help me carry these things out to the car. We'll take Michael home."

No one argued when Mama was set on something.

"You boys stay here in the car. I'll be back in a jiffy," she said when we got to Michael's house.

Mama waltzed up the front steps of the old Wilson place like it was a fancy hotel instead of a ramshackle old house. Michael sat stony-faced and still, except for his feet, which kept bouncing off the floor of the car like they were about to run down the road. You could feel the ache coming off that boy, how bad he wanted to keep those clothes, and how afraid he was that his pa and ma were going to say, "No."

"Good afternoon, folks. I'm Mary, your neighbor down the road a bit. I am so sorry for bothering you, but I wanted to talk to you about something..."

We didn't hear the rest of it because Michael's parents suddenly remembered their manners and invited Mama into the house.

Pretty soon, Mama came out to the car, Michael's daddy trailing behind her.

"I appreciate this," Mama told him. "I'm glad Michael can get some use out of these things." Mama smiled, and the warmth of that smile lit up the day like sunshine after a cold spring rain.

"Missus, we surely do thank you," Michael's daddy said, and Michael let out a long, breathless sigh.

The next day, Michael was a new boy, tall and proud. His clothes were crisp and clean, and so was he. He must have spent hours scrubbing the dirt out from under his fingernails. No one said a word to him about wearing Ambrose's old shoes and coat. It was like Ambrose cast a magic spell and turned Michael into a real boy.

Day after day, Michael kept himself and his clothes clean. Then, just a few months later, Michael's pa found a real good job downstate. Michael cried when he came to say good-bye.

I thought Ambrose would feel bad when Michael left.

"You're going to miss him, aren't you?" I asked him one day while we were out in the yard playing catch.

"Yeah, I am, but I'm glad for him, too. He deserved a lot better than the old Wilson place on Cabbage Road," he said, and he meant it.

Ambrose was just that way. He made things better than they were when he found them. At least, he used to.

Sometimes I think I dreamed up that whole other family, our whole other life. There's a family portrait hanging on the wall in the living room. Mama and Daddy are sitting down in the picture and me and Ambrose are standing up behind them. Ambrose just told us a silly joke about a talking dog at a picnic, and Mama's eyes are twinkling. You can tell it's her real, honest-to-goodness smile, not one of those stupid "everyone-say-cheese" smiles. It's a happy smile. The kind of smile that doesn't know in six months she and Ambrose are going to wreck the car. She doesn't know Ambrose is going to shatter his leg and hit his head when the car slams into a tree, or how he's not going to wake up again for two whole weeks. Thankfully, Mama doesn't know she'll be gone and buried by then and, in a way, that Ambrose will die that day, too.

The boy who woke up isn't anything like the Ambrose smiling in the picture. He's a stranger, mean and cold and angry, and he doesn't remember the accident. There's a lot he doesn't remember, like all those stupid jokes he liked to tell. Mama won't know how sometimes Ambrose sits on his bed and tries to remember the boy he used to be, a boy who's gone and lost to us now. No, none of us could have guessed any of that as we were sitting there smiling into the photographer's lights.

The house was cold when I finally got home. Daddy wasn't there, which was kind of a mixed blessing. He wasn't there to shout and yell and cuff us if we got too close or if we did something he didn't like, like not getting the dishes done or not having supper on the table. But then, there was the worry. What trouble was he in now?

Once, right after Mama died, the sheriff brought Daddy home. He'd found Daddy passed out cold alongside his truck in the parking lot of a roadhouse outside of town. Sheriff Miller helped me haul Daddy to his bed.

"I'm sorry for your troubles, son. Your mama was a fine woman and y'all have been through a rough time," the big man told me. "But I catch your pa driving drunk, he's going to jail. You tell him I said so in the morning when he sobers up."

"Yes, sir."

The sheriff looked like he wanted to say more, but whatever was on his mind, he let it rest. The police car's taillights disappeared into the night, and I worried about what would happen next time. After that, Daddy took care not to drive if he'd been drinking. Sometimes we didn't see him for days.

I opened a can of stew and picked up the house while the food was heating. Most of the stuff lying around was Ambrose's. I hung up his coat and moved his shoes from the middle of the doorway. Then I picked up his school books and headed to his room.

"Get out." His voice was low. He was lying on his bed in the dark.

"I got your stuff here. You need to put it away before Daddy comes home."

"Okay," came his muffled voice, and then I realized Ambrose was crying. I slunk out of his room and shut the door as quiet as I could, shaking like a newborn foal. I'd never seen Ambrose cry, not even in the hospital when Daddy told him about Mama. Ambrose *never* cried.

Once, when we were little, we'd taken a stick and aggravated a nest of hornets. The angry bugs came after us like demons, stinging both of us until we were hurt and swelled up like Mama's red pin cushion. I wailed so loud and so long, Mama said she thought it was the Second Coming. Ambrose, who had taken the brunt of it trying to keep the hornets off me, sat quiet, red, and swollen, not a single tear in his eyes.

Now, he sobbed like his heart was broken, hoarse, ragged cries that hurt to hear. I covered my ears. He was like a wounded animal, and I thought of the cat. I felt empty and sick inside and scared. I didn't know what to do, so I turned off the stew and sat on the back steps, hoping Daddy would come home, hoping he'd be sober, and praying he'd know what to do for Ambrose.

Something moved. I saw it out of the corner of my eye. It was the cat, the stupid, lame cat. He was just begging for trouble tonight.

"Get!" I cried. "Get out of here!"

The cat froze in the darkness.

"Don't," Ambrose called down from his bedroom window. "Don't scare it, Tom. I'm comin' down."

A terrible thought crept into my mind. What if Ambrose was coming down to kill the cat? He tried to hurt it every time he saw the pitiful thing. If anyone knew about hurting, it was Ambrose. I knew then that I wouldn't let him hurt the cat again. I couldn't stand it.

The screen door squeaked, and the cat jumped at the noise, but didn't run. Maybe it couldn't.

"It's okay," Ambrose said, his voice all silky and smooth. He crept softly through the wet grass, closer and closer to the cat.

I stood up, not sure what to do.

"Ambrose," I whispered, "please don't hurt him."

I didn't know if he heard me or not.

"If he hurts the cat again," I thought, "then I know the Ambrose I love is gone for good." I couldn't bear to watch, but I couldn't turn away.

Off in the distance, a train whistle blew, lonesome and mournful, like the cry the cat made when Ambrose hit him with the rock. The haunting sound floated on the night, and Ambrose stopped and cocked his head, listening. So did the cat. I held my breath.

Ambrose reached down and lifted the cat up into his arms. My heart hammered like it was trying to burst right out of my chest. I opened my mouth, but no sound came out. Then Ambrose buried his face in the cat's filthy fur.

"I'm sorry," he cried hoarsely, saying the words over and over. "I'm so sorry."

Like a sleepwalker waking up from a deep and complicated dream, I shook myself. The next thing I knew, I was standing in the yard holding my big brother, Ambrose, in the circle of my arms. Both of us were crying, and the cat, the stupid, three-legged cat, trapped between the two of us, was purring.

We walked back inside the house and Ambrose took a careful look at the cat, prodding here and there. For his part, the cat was pretty cooperative considering his history with Ambrose.

Then Ambrose and I gave the cat a bath. It sounds easy enough, but let me tell you, I'd rather face another round of angry hornets than try to bathe the cat again. It was all we could do to keep him in the sink long enough to wash the dirt and grime out of his fur. He fought like a lion. Twice he escaped, and we chased him, slick and sudsy, through the house.

When we were done and exhausted, Ambrose dried him gently with one of Mama's good towels. Somehow it seemed right, and I don't think Mama would have minded.

Ambrose sat at the table brushing the cat's fur until it was silky and dry. The cat's tail, soft as summer dandelions, wound itself through the air, touching Ambrose's face now and then. A lump rose in my throat. As the cat's fur dried, it turned a burnished brown, the same beautiful color as Mama's hair. Watching Ambrose, so gentle with the cat, I felt like, at long last, my big brother was home.

We talked late into the night about Mama and Daddy, about the accident, even about the cat, who shared our stew and ended up asleep on Ambrose's lap.

"It was my fault, Tom. Mama was taking me to town. A deer ran in front of the car." Silent tears streamed down his face.

"When did you remember?"

"A couple of days ago. It was all my fault." He wiped at the tears with the back of his hand.

"How is it your fault, Ambrose? How can a car wreck be your fault?"

"Don't you see, Tom? I begged Mama to go to town that day. She wanted to wait until Saturday, have Daddy drive us, but I wouldn't wait. I wanted to get us a real bat. I made Mama go to town, pleading and begging 'til I wore her down. If I'd only waited like she wanted, she'd still be alive."

His voice cracked and more tears came. It was like a lifetime of not crying had suddenly caught up with him.

I covered his hand with mine.

"Ambrose, it isn't your fault. You know how Mama was. Mama did what Mama wanted to do. She wouldn't have driven that day if she didn't want to. If you want to blame someone, blame the deer for running across the road. Then blame the sun for rising and the moon for setting. Accidents happen, Ambrose, it wasn't your fault!"

It was a long speech for me, but Ambrose seemed to find some comfort in it. His fingers made slow, lazy circles in the cat's soft fur. The cat moaned a little, and then let out a short snore. Ambrose and I burst out laughing. The cat raised its sleepy head and then nestled farther down into Ambrose's lap.

"What are we going to do about Daddy?" Ambrose asked after a while.

"I don't know," I answered truthfully, but I felt a flicker of hope. Maybe, now that Ambrose was back, Daddy would get better. Maybe we could be happy again and go back to being a family. Ambrose always had a way of making things better.

Sitting there at the table, listening to the cat purr, the cat that could forgive Ambrose, I thought maybe there was hope for us yet.

Tyler at Camp Amigo
Monica Clark

Tyler Spencer had a problem. Not your average, everyday kind of problem like oversleeping or finding out that his little brother spilled orange juice all over his math homework. No, Tyler Spencer had a bigger problem.

Every year for as long as anyone could remember, the sixth-graders of Westview Elementary School went to Camp Amigo. The camp was a wondrous place where students camped, fished, canoed, took nature hikes, went to cooking classes, and ended each night sitting around a roaring campfire. The ghost stories told around those fires were legendary. Many a shivering camper spent the night bolt upright in bed, flashlight gripped tightly in hand, anxiously waiting for the first sign of dawn.

No one, no one, wanted to miss the trip to Camp Amigo. Well, almost no one. One student, one particular student named Tyler Spencer, did not want to go.

It wasn't the teacher assigned to the cabin that made Tyler quiver in fear. Although, if the truth be told, Mr. Flora was quite frightening. You would think a man whose name meant "flower" would be tiny, pleasant and dainty, but Mr. Flora was the complete opposite of all those things. He was a giant of a man who lifted weights and coached the football team at the local high school. A huge, hulking figure with a bald head, a great, black, bushy beard and a no-nonsense outlook on life. He never laughed, and when Mr. Flora bellowed, which he did frequently, windows rattled, cars screeched to a halt, and dogs howled in terror, tucked tail and ran. No, believe it or not, it wasn't Mr.

Flora that caused Tyler to tremble at the thought of visiting Camp Amigo. Tyler had a bigger problem than that.

Nor was it his roommate assignment that put him off going to camp. Ben Landon was his best friend, and Tyler loved the idea of partnering and sharing a cabin with him. Ben was the only person who knew Tyler's deepest, darkest secret.

His problem? Tyler Spencer was a sleepwalker. Not your ordinary, everyday kind sleepwalker. Tyler was an *imaginative* sleepwalker. Once he dreamed he was fishing in a pond and awoke to find himself wearing his old fishing hat, pajama bottoms wet with dew, casting flies into his next-door neighbor's swimming pool.

More than once, he found himself dreaming about going to the bathroom and woke up to find himself watering the kitchen trashcan, or worse, his mother's lush, green philodendron. The philodendron incident would not have been so bad, except the plant sat on a table right in front of the living room window. When Tyler woke up, he looked out the window and found the paperboy staring at him in shocked horror, still clutching the morning news. Tyler yanked down the shade and vowed never to tell his mother what happened to her favorite plant.

Just a week later, Tyler dreamed he was flying. When he awoke, he really was flying. Somehow, he left the house and pushed his bike up the notoriously steep Dead Man's Hill. In his sleep, he managed to make it almost all the way down the dangerous mountain road, but his waking self panicked. The bike's handlebars wobbled, and Tyler knew he was doomed. At the last possible moment, he saw a giant haystack just off the asphalt near the bottom of Dead Man's Hill. He aimed for it and closed his eyes.

Wind whooshed and whistled by his ears, but all Tyler heard was his own long and drawn-out scream. With a giant "whoomf," the speeding bike plunged deep inside the dry, itchy stack. Gasping for breath, Tyler was surprised to find he was still alive.

When his heart stopped racing, he dug himself out and he and the bike wobbled home.

"What is all of this?" his mother demanded the next morning, staring at the trail of hay leading up to his bed.

"I must have skipped my shower last night," he offered weakly.

"Well, young man, you are not going out today until you clean up this mess," she ordered.

"There is no way I'm going to Camp Amigo," Tyler muttered as he changed the sheets. He could only imagine what might happen if his sleepwalking kicked in at camp. It was social suicide. He decided to talk to Mr. Flora the following Monday.

"Not going? Not going? What do you mean, you're not going?" Mr. Flora bellowed, towering over Tyler like a giant ogre or a cave troll.

"Well ... it's ... um ... I just ..." but Tyler never got the chance to finish his sentence.

"You are going, Spencer, even if I have to drag you there by your heels! This is a school activity, and I am not going to tolerate a whiney little slacker on my watch! Get used to the idea, Spencer, you're going!"

Mr. Flora stomped out of the room, and Tyler felt like a bug smashed into a speeding windshield.

"Look, Ty, you'll be fine. We just have to come up with a plan," Ben tried to console him.

Ben thought for a minute. "Hey, I've got it." He grinned. "Don't go to sleep! We'll really only be there four nights. You can stay awake that long, can't you?"

"Stay awake four nights? Are you kidding? No one can stay awake that long!"

"Well, it's not like we're going to be getting a lot of sleep anyway. My brother said when he went to camp, most nights he didn't hit the sack until after midnight. Even if you do fall asleep, you'll be too tired to sleepwalk."

A small bit of hope glimmered, a bit like a firefly on the last night of summer, and Tyler gave into it. "Do you really think it will work?"

"I know it will," Ben said. "Steve said they were up before sunrise every day. When he came home, he collapsed on the couch and snored like a lumberjack for the next twelve hours. He didn't even eat supper that night. Ty, I guarantee you, it'll work."

✧

And that is how Tyler Spencer, sleepwalker extraordinaire, found himself standing in a cabin at Camp Amigo a week later.

"You take the top bunk, Ty. That way if you, ah, you know what, I'll wake up and stop you," Ben said quietly.

"I sure hope this plan of yours works. Otherwise, I'll have to run away and join the circus or something."

Ben laughed. "No need to do that. I won't let you down. Trust me, Ty. What can go wrong?"

The campers unpacked their gear. Tyler and Ben's bunks were attached to the back wall.

"Good," Tyler thought, "the farther away from the door, the better."

He carefully hid his i-Pod under a pillow. The camp had a stern "no electronics" policy, but Tyler was sure in this instance, it was better to break the rule than to end up sleepwalking. The music player was loaded with band and techno music, all of it loud, jarring, and certain to keep Tyler awake while the other campers slept. He and Ben loaded it with sound effects, too: chainsaws, diesel engines, whistles, bells, the wailing of a flock of peacocks at the zoo, and a hundred alarm clocks all going off at once. And, if that wasn't enough, they even included the "1812 Overture," complete with the sound of cannon fire. The stay-awake plan had to work.

And it worked perfectly until halfway through the night. Tyler's eyelids felt like lead weights. Twice, he felt himself nodding off, so he cranked up the volume on his i-Pod so loud his ears rang. Somehow, Tyler managed to stay awake the rest of the night. He zombie-walked through most of the next day, but he made it.

Unfortunately, by the time his head hit the pillow that night, the i-Pod was useless. Ben was no help either. He was asleep before Tyler made it all the way up into his bunk. The "1812 Overture" may as well have been a lullaby, and soon every camper in Cabin Seven was sound asleep.

Tyler was dreaming. He was paddling a canoe with Ben. Rise and dip, rise and dip, the paddle went up and down. Suddenly, a wailing scream disturbed his sleep. At first, Tyler thought it was the peacocks from the i-Pod. He smiled, glad to discover the plan was working. Then he opened his eyes and found himself standing waist-deep in the lake, canoe paddle in hand.

"Ghost!" Someone on shore pointed at him and another scream echoed across the lake. Tyler dove under the water, holding his breath as long as he could. When he popped up again, gasping for air, the beach looked deserted.

In his dream, Tyler had been paddling a canoe on a warm, sunny day; he was standing in cold water wearing only his underwear, holding a wooden paddle and paddling an imaginary canoe. Fog floated over the lake, and his pasty, white, goose-bump-covered skin seemed to glow in the moonlight.

A scream echoed across the water. "Run!"

Squinting through the fog, Tyler saw the disappearing shape of two girls from his class. He hurried to shore, found his pajamas and scurried back to his snug, dry cabin. As the girls' cabins lit up one by one, back in his bunk, a very exhausted Tyler Spencer fell asleep.

"Hey, did you hear what happened last night?" one of the boys asked at breakfast. "Some of the girls saw a ghost out on the lake!"

It was only then that Tyler remembered sleepwalking. Ben and Tyler eyed each other.

"Dude, was that you?" Ben whispered.

Tyler nodded. "What happened to the plan?" he asked sullenly. "I thought you were supposed to help me stay awake."

"Gosh, Ty, I'm sorry. It's harder than I thought."

"Tell me about it!" Tyler snapped.

By lunchtime, the story had grown. It was now an established fact. A new legend was born that day—an urban legend about a boy who died in a terrible canoeing accident whose lonely ghost now haunted Camp Amigo.

"Some people are so gullible," Ben said, laughing.

"Thank goodness," Ty said, and the two headed off to campfire cooking class.

That evening, fireflies flickered like golden eyes in the woods. With no flashlights, only the light of a full moon lit the trail as the night hike began. The ranger who guided them deep into the forest was a young college student working for the camp that summer. He led them along a quiet trail softened by pine needles, pausing every so often to point out something interesting. Mr. Flora brought up the rear.

"Listen," the ranger said as they stopped by a misty marsh along the edge of the forest.

"Barrummph, Barrummph, barrummph." The sound was loud in the stillness.

"Can anyone tell me what that is?" the ranger asked.

"A bird?" guessed one of the girls.

"No."

"My sister?" Ben offered, jabbing Tyler in the ribs.

"Knock it off, Landon," Mr. Flora bellowed, and for a moment the entire forest was silent.

Finally, the "barrummph" sounded again.

"Is it the ghost?" whispered Sylvia Johnson, one of the girls who stumbled upon Tyler the night before.

"Hardly," laughed the ranger. "No, folks, that is the sound of an American bullfrog. C'mon, let's keep going."

The hike seemed to last for hours, and soon Tyler and other campers were yawning.

"We'll take a break up here in a little clearing," the ranger said.

"Yay," someone said half-heartedly.

The group rested on a patch of soft grass, sitting on or leaning against sections of logs spread out in a circle. Little clouds of night mist settled around the low spots and drifted into the forest. Tyler started thinking of a movie he saw once about a werewolf that threatened a small English village. He glanced up at the full moon and yawned.

The ranger's voice droned on and on. He talked about crickets and salamanders, owls and foxes, predators and prey, and food chains and before he knew it, Tyler dozed off. As he fell asleep, almost instantly, he began dreaming he was a werewolf.

Ben, who was dozing, shook himself, and suddenly realized Tyler was gone.

"Dude, where are you?" he whispered.

There was a rustling in the leaves, and Ben was relieved. Tyler was not far away. Ben slipped away from the group, crawling on hands and knees toward the rustling sound.

He was nearly there when a long, bone-chilling howl erupted from the woods. The wail bounced off the treetops and the sound was everywhere at once. The ranger stopped mid-sentence, and the entire group turned, facing the woods. It was then that a giant, shadowy, manlike figure arose from the depths of the forest.

Everything happened at once. A flock of birds nestled in the trees above the clearing took off. Their wing beats and squawks added to the din. A herd of deer bedded down in a nearby meadow took flight, snorting and thumping, hoof beats thundering. The young ranger screamed and ran away.

Another howl from the dark figure shattered the night, and even though Ben knew it was Tyler, an icy chill shivered its way up his spine. For the other campers, it was far worse.

Mr. Flora shot up off his log. He tripped and fell down over the log, sending it and himself rolling. Then, he jumped up again, squealing like a hog headed for market. Had there been a hair left on his shiny, bald head, it surely would have stood at attention. Another shrill scream erupted from the giant man, and he turned and ran crashing through the brush in the opposite direction. A moment later, remembering he was a teacher, he stopped for a second and yelled, "Run! Run for your lives!" Then the big man fled, racing toward the cabins.

And run they did. Screams, shrieks, yells and howls rent the night. Ben was the only camper still in the clearing.

"Ty? Ty, where are you?" he called.

"I'm here."

"Follow my voice," Ben said.

The bushes shook, and Tyler stumbled into the clearing.

"C'mon," Ben urged, "we've got to get back to camp before someone figures out what happened."

The two boys jogged along the empty path back to their cabin.

No one slept that night. For the first time in its history, the doors at Camp Amigo were locked. No one went out alone, and every light in every building was on all night long.

Sunrise brought sanity back to camp. A zoologist from the State arrived. He and Mr. Flora went into the woods to look for tracks. There was talk of Bigfoot and bears or maybe an escaped gorilla, but, of course, nothing was found. Activities resumed, except for the night hike.

Morning turned into afternoon, and afternoon turned into the last night at Camp Amigo.

"We made it," Ben said sleepily, climbing into his bunk. "I've still got your back, Ty," he added, yawning.

"I hope so, Ben, I hope so," Tyler said, his eyes closing as soon as his head hit the pillow.

Tyler Spencer slept long into the night. Ben and the other boys of Cabin Seven gave into their weariness. Mr. Flora, having regained some of his dignity during the day, snored loud and deep.

Tyler was dreaming he was at the pet shop. His mother said he could pick out any animal he wanted. He looked at dogs, cats, parrots and ferrets, and finally decided on a cute little black and white kitten. The kitten was larger than the others, but Tyler liked it best. He fell into a deep and dreamless sleep with a smile on his face.

Ben woke up at sunrise. The other campers were still asleep. Only Mr. Flora's bunk was empty. He often got up early to take his shower before the other campers were up and around. Ben stared at the bunk above his and smiled. Ty was still in bed. No sleepwalking for him.

"We did it," Ben whispered. "We made it."

"Help," a strangled cry came from above.

"What's wrong?" Ben sat up quickly.

"Stop," Ty commanded. "Don't shake the bunk."

"What?" Ben asked, rubbing his eyes.

"Help me," came the plea from the upper bunk

Ben crept out of bed and slowly made his way up the ladder to Ty's bunk. Tyler was still wrapped up in his sleeping bag, but nestled against his stomach, snoring softly, was a dark, furry shape.

"Hey, dude, where'd you get the cat?" Ben asked.

At the sound of Ben's voice, the animal moaned in its sleep and rolled over. It was only then that Ben realized Tyler was spooning the biggest skunk he had ever seen.

"How...?" Ben covered his mouth as the skunk moaned again.

"What am I going to do?" Ty whispered.

"How did you ... what did you..." Ben could not formulate a thought. He shook himself. Tyler was his friend. He tried to think.

"Okay. What if I pull you and the sleeping bag off the end of the bunk?" he whispered. "You think you can get out that way?"

"We can try," Ty said. "But first I have to move my arm. He's sleeping on it."

"Okay, just be careful."

"I am," Tyler hissed.

"Oh boy, here we go." Ben took a deep breath and held it.

Inch by inch, Tyler pulled his arm out from under the sleeping animal. The skunk moved once and then curled into a ball.

"Whew, that was close," Ben whispered.

"Yeah, but we're not out of the woods yet," Tyler whispered.

"Look around, dude, we are totally in the woods."

"Funny," Ty snapped.

Moving glacier-slow, Ben pulled Ty and the nylon sleeping bag toward the edge of the bed.

"Take my hand. Now, take it slow and easy," Ben said.

Tyler moved as if his life depended on it, because technically it did; his social life, anyway. He slid out of the bed in slow motion. When he was halfway down the bunk, hanging over the edge, the skunk groaned and opened its eyes. Both boys froze.

The uninvited guest stretched to its full length and lay on the bed with all four paws in the air. Sweat dropped off the tip of Tyler's nose and an eternity seemed to pass before the skunk's soft snores started again.

Tyler climbed down the ladder like a mountaineer descending the heights of Mount Everest. An eternity later, he and the sleeping bag landed on the floor.

"Thanks, Ben. You saved my life," he said, fighting the urge to hug his friend.

"No big deal. Now, let's wake up the guys and get out of here."

Quietly, they woke their fellow campers. The boys of Cabin Seven were huddled together outside the door, shivering in the cool morning air, when Mr. Flora marched up and pushed his way through the group. He was shirtless, dressed in tiny gym shorts, with a towel slung around his neck.

"What is going on here?" he yelled, bursting through the cabin door.

A chorus of voices arose.

"Mr. Flora..."

"Wait!"

"I wouldn't do that..."

"I don't know what you boys think you're up to," he yelled, and pushed his way further into the cabin.

"Who let the cat in here?" Mr. Flora bellowed.

In horror, the boys of Cabin Seven watched Mr. Flora snatch the sleeping skunk off the bed.

Holding it by the scruff of its neck, Mr. Flora began, "We don't allow pets at camp, you..."

It was unclear how Mr. Flora intended to finish his sentence. However, the skunk made it very clear how he felt about being woken up so abruptly.

Time seemed to slow, and then a cloying stench suddenly blossomed from the cabin, followed by a strangled, "Arrgggghhhhhh!"

Mr. Flora burst out of the cabin, scattering the boys like a bowling ball plowing through pins. The boys separated and let him pass. Mr. Flora raced to the lake, screaming like a banshee, scrubbing his face, neck and chest with lake water and sand.

"Pee uuu," Ben said, plugging his nose.

The group shrank away from the stinking shack.

A crowd gathered to watch Mr. Flora as the giant man dove under the water over and over again, trying to rid himself of a face full of skunk.

For his part, the skunk ambled away from the cabin and slowly headed back into the woods.

"How did you ever manage to get that thing into your bunk?" Ben asked quietly.

"Dunno," Tyler said. "But, I have to say, I'm glad this is the last day of Camp Amigo."

"Yeah, me too."

In the years that followed, that particular week at Camp Amigo was legendary. New campers were warned of the dangers of the ghost in the lake, the monster in the woods and the amazing bunk-climbing skunks that inhabited the camp.

Tyler, with the help of his good friend, Ben, survived his time at camp with his reputation intact. All in all, it was a good trip.

For Mr. Flora, it was something more. After missing nearly a week of school while waiting for the odor of skunk to wear off, a most amazing change came over Mr. Flora. He stopped coaching football and took up gardening. His flowers were so beautiful that they won awards. He became kinder and gentler, and he no longer bellowed. And, he never, ever went back to Camp Amigo.

Morning on the River
Monica Clark

"Be careful, Madi, the rocks are slippery," Dad says, and the bright-red canoe wobbles as I scramble into it. He hands me a short wooden paddle and pushes us away from shore.

We glide through soft clouds of floating fog, and the gray-green water shimmers, glass-smooth and still. A loon wails its lonely, quavering song, and the sound bounces through the gathering mist. Along the shore, tall and slender cattails grow both up and down in the water's mirror.

The boat slips silently through the water. We paddle along the curve of a small peninsula and I see something moving.

"Raccoon," Dad says quietly.

As we close in, the furry gray bandit spots us and freezes, crouching on the trunk of a fallen willow. Then he waddles away, chortling and scolding us for interrupting his day. Dad and I laugh.

"Knee-deep, knee-deep!" a frog laughs with us from the reeds.

Around the bend, a heron hunts for breakfast in the shallows. His long, pointed beak darts suddenly into the water. His curvy neck straightens as he slowly swallows a fish. Huge wings open slowly and he flies away, soaring above the ribbon of river.

Our paddles rise and dip, rise and dip, as the sun climbs higher and higher, burning away the mist.

"See that, Madi?" Dad asks.

I see it and grab the empty pop bottle as we pass. I set it in the bottom of the boat, and Dad nods.

"Here we are," he says when we reach a small, quiet cove. He picks up a blue rope and gently slides the anchor overboard. Then he hands me my fishing pole.

"I'll put on the first worm, Madi, and after that, it's up to you."

My first cast is jerky, but the worm stays on, and the red and white bobber settles in the water. Dad's cast is smooth. His bobber plunks close to mine.

The morning fog is gone completely. Seagulls fly lazy circles overhead. Squawking loudly, they turn and wheel away. A soft breeze begins to blow, shattering the sunlight on the water into a million shining stars.

"Madi!" Dad yells.

My bobber is gone, pulled under when I wasn't looking. I yank up on the pole, but I am too late. The small gold hook is bare. Now it's my turn to bait the hook. I pick up a worm, trying hard not to make a face.

The reel whirs, and the line sails through the air as I cast out again.

Now Dad has a bite. He pulls in a fat sunfish, and then another, and another.

Finally, my bobber jiggles. This time I'm ready. Another sunfish flashes out of the water.

"Good job," Dad says, and I feel his smile.

Gentle waves rock the boat, and the sun warms my back like a soft blanket.

"Well, Madi," Dad says after a while, "it's about time we head back."

He pulls in his line while I cast out one more time.

My bobber doesn't land. It dives deep under the water. I am so surprised, I forget to move.

"Madi!" Dad yells.

I lift the pole, and it bends almost in half.

"What do you have, Madi?"

"I don't know, but it's big!"

I turn the silver crank as fast as I can, but the reel squeals, and the line goes out again.

"Dad, what do I do?" I yell.

"Stay calm, Madi, just keep reeling. Let the pole do the work."

I pull up on the pole, but the fish swims harder. My hands are hot and sweating. Then the fish swirls close to the boat. I can see it.

The big fish dives one more time, and then comes up alongside the boat, too tired to fight anymore.

She's a bass, big and beautiful, with a dark stripe running down both sides. Her belly is white and plump and full of eggs. She opens her mouth wide, trying to spit out the hook, and her gills gleam silver-green in the clear water. Marble-sized black eyes watch me. She is the biggest fish I have ever caught. She is the biggest fish I have ever seen.

We all seem frozen in that moment. Dad watches me. I watch the bass.

"I can't wait to show Mom," I say, my heart singing. And then it hits me. She is full of eggs. There is only one thing to do.

"Madi," Dad begins, "You can't..."

"I know, Dad," I tell him before he can finish, "I know. She belongs in the river."

"That's right," he says, and carefully he unhooks my bass. She hovers near the canoe, not knowing she is free. Then, with a swish of her tail, she disappears. My big fish is gone.

I try hard to swallow the lump in my throat.

The canoe dips as Dad leans forward and puts his hand on my shoulder.

"Madi, I'm proud of you. I couldn't have done any better myself."

I smile, and the tight spot in my throat disappears. A warm feeling settles in its place.

"C'mon." Dad grins, lifting the anchor. "Let's go tell your mom."

We paddle back to camp, and I think about the raccoon and the heron. I think about the sunfish and the morning mist. I even think about those seagulls whirling and twirling in the sky. But mostly, I think about my bass. Somewhere in the cool water, she is searching for a safe place to lay her eggs. Her babies will hatch and a whole new group of tiny fish will find their place in the river.

Mom waves from shore, and I wave back. I can hardly wait to tell her about morning on the river.

You Make Your Choices
Monica Clark

I was pissed. No reason to sugarcoat it. Two miles past livid. Deep into the realm of murderously angry. I should have known. Todd was so antsy on the long drive up to the cabin, I should have known. It wasn't until I heard the dull "thump, thump" of a too-loud stereo that I put it together.

"What *is* that?" I asked, hoping against hope the familiar obnoxious booming was a Forest Service helicopter.

My husband shrugged and stalked outside, slamming the door behind him.

"Todd?"

He didn't answer, and the Chevy Camaro fish-tailing up the dusty lane was the only answer I needed.

"What is going on?" I asked, stomping down the stairs. "What are they doing here?"

Todd wouldn't look at me.

"It's okay, babe. I invited them," he mumbled.

"You what?" I roared with righteous indignation. "You invited them? To our cabin? Our vacation? You invited them?"

Jason Warner, a complete waste of humanity, and his pale, skinny sidekick, Mark, grinned up at me through the windshield. Jason, swaggering and greasy-haired, was somehow under the mistaken impression he was God's gift to women. His brand of charm was totally wasted on me, but that didn't stop him from trying. Todd brought him to the house a few months ago and they spent the evening drinking beer in the garage. When Todd came in to use the bathroom, Jason cornered me in my kitchen.

"Hey, pretty lady, how are you doing?" He came up behind me and pressed himself against me. I pushed him and tried to slip away, but he grabbed my wrists hard enough to leave bruises.

"Don't be shy," he said, laughing.

"Let me go," I told him.

"What if I don't?" he asked, squeezing my wrists harder and pushing himself against me again.

"Todd!" I shouted, and Jason let me go.

"Just trying to be friendly," Jason said smoothly.

Later, when I told Todd what he had done, Todd laughed, actually laughed.

"Don't worry, babe. He's alright."

"Todd, I don't think you understand. Your friend assaulted me."

"Babe, you're really blowing this out of proportion. He's a little rough, but you'll like him once you know him better."

I did not want to know him any better. I loathed the man, and now here he was driving up the lane.

"I thought he was in jail," I said.

"No, he caught up on his child support. It's okay, babe, really."

The car slammed to a stop in a cloud of dust, just inches from the back stairs of the cabin. The passenger side door flew open, and an empty beer can rolled out and fell to the ground.

"Oops!" Mark said, fumbling his way out of the car. Then he doubled over and threw up.

"Are you kidding me?" I hissed at Todd.

Jason poured himself out of the driver's side door and slammed his hand on top of the car.

"Damn, buddy, you weren't lying. This is the middle of nowhere."

I couldn't even look at them. I didn't know who I was madder at, them or Todd.

"Todd's going through a phase," I had kidded myself for a long time. It was a phase, alright, a second adolescence for a man who still had roots dug firmly in the first. It was clear to me that Todd was not the same man I married five years ago. Pride kept me there, but even that was wearing thin. This was just too much.

It was supposed to be our vacation, even though Todd hadn't worked in over six months. I had put in double shifts at work, sixteen hours some days, for weeks. I was exhausted, physically and emotionally. I needed this time away.

I hoped Todd and I could repair some of the awful things we'd said to each other lately. But hope hadn't gotten me much—thirty-seven years old and married to a man I couldn't trust, a man who would invite scum like Jason up to my special place. Todd and I spent our honeymoon here at the cabin.

Mama and Daddy used to take me and Carole up to the cabin when we were little. I was five years old the first time I saw the place, and I was frightened. The forest was dark and terrible, and the trees seemed to creep up on the cabin, but after a few years, I fell in love with its tranquil beauty.

Our cabin started out as the home of the superintendent of a quarrying operation about four miles down the road. The quarry was the area's only source of livelihood until workers punched into an underground aquifer. Twelve men died, and the company spent a small fortune trying to stem the flow of water, but in the end, nature won out. The quarry flooded, and the company went bankrupt. Most of the land was sold to the State for pennies, but my father bought the cabin. Daddy left it to me when he died.

I was twelve years old the last time Mama and Daddy brought us here. Daddy took us to see the quarry that last summer before Carole got sick.

"What are they doing here?" Daddy frowned at a group of teenage boys whooping and diving off the quarry's steep, stony cliffs.

"Daddy, can we go swimming?" Carole asked.

"No, honey," he said. "It's not safe."

"But they're swimming," Carole whined, pointing to the laughing teenagers.

"They shouldn't be," Daddy said. "It's dangerous."

One boy, tall and tanned, walked to the edge of the cliff. Just before he dove, he turned, looked at me, and waved. I watched him disappear into the cold, black water, and my flesh broke out in goosebumps.

"Daddy, can we go, please? Let's go back!" I begged.

The water was dark and forbidding, but worse, it looked *hungry*. I started to cry.

"Honey, what's the matter?" Daddy asked, frowning at the boys in the water.

"I don't know," I sobbed. "I just want to go."

"Okay, sweetie, we'll head back."

We walked to the car and Daddy drove us back to the cabin.

A few hours later, we heard the sirens. The wind carried the sound for miles. Daddy hopped in the car to see what was happening. When he came back, his face was grey.

"Honey, what is it?" Mama clutched at his arm. "Are you alright?"

"Yes, Clara, I'm fine. It was those kids, they were just kids..." His voice cracked and he turned away.

The low murmur of voices woke me later that night. I crept out, hiding in the shadows of the living room. Mama and Daddy sat huddled together on the front porch. Moonlight turned the lake silver.

"The sheriff said they'll probably never find the bodies."

"Hush, Marvin, you don't need to keep going over this. It's not your fault."

"Clara, if I had run them off, they'd still be alive. Two kids died this afternoon, and I could have stopped it." His voice rose.

"Shh, you'll wake the girls. Listen to me. Those kids chose to swim where it was unsafe. They made a choice, and it turned out badly. They were young and foolish. You make your choices, and then you live with them."

Daddy began to cry.

"Hey, it's okay," Mama soothed. She held his head, and gently rocked him just like she did when Carole or I fell and skinned a knee. It hurt to see my Daddy so upset, and I hurried back to bed and hid under the covers, sweating until I fell asleep.

On the way home, Daddy stopped in Newburg, about forty miles from the cabin, and bought a newspaper. The front page screamed the story.

"According to witnesses, fifteen-year-old Timothy McMichael dove into the water and when he failed to surface, seventeen-year-old Darrin Carter jumped in after him. Neither boy surfaced again."

The two boys looked up from grainy photographs on the front page, and I recognized the boy who smiled and waved at me before diving off the cliff. Daddy folded the paper and slid it under the seat. He gave Mama a funny look, his knuckles white as he clutched the Plymouth's steering wheel. Slowly, he turned the key. The old Fury sparked to life, and we headed home.

Carole died of leukemia the next summer. There were mountains of medical bills, and as far as I know, Daddy never visited the cabin again.

"Your father always blamed himself for those kids dying, you know," Mama told me years later. A few months after Daddy died, I was helping her box up his things and found the newspaper in his desk drawer, yellow and stiff with age.

"They never found those poor boys."

"What do you mean they never found them?" I asked.

"Well, your father followed the story for weeks. They dragged the quarry, even used explosives to try to loosen up any snags. Nothing worked. Those poor boys."

I remembered the hungry water and shivered at the idea of the bodies still down there, held tight in the water's dark embrace.

"Swallowed up whole," I thought suddenly, and that's just how I felt now, swallowed up whole. My life with Todd was a dark hole with a strong current pulling me down.

I was thirty-two and not getting any younger when I married Todd. None of my friends

liked him. He was brash and young, only twenty-five, but he treated me well. He was

good-looking and so charming. Where was that man now? I knew that coming up to the cabin

was our last chance to see if there was anything worth salvaging.

I stormed up the steps and slammed the cabin door behind me.

"Old lady pissed at ya, Buddy?" Jason said. Whatever my husband answered made the men laugh.

I fled to the front porch, panting with impotent rage. The lake, calm and blue, sparkled and beckoned, but did nothing to change my mood. I was too far gone. I had to do something before I exploded, so I started running. I raced down to the lake, out to the end of the shaky pier, and threw myself in the water. It was shockingly cold. So cold it took my breath away, like a slap in the face. It was just what I needed.

I swam until I was exhausted, then I pulled myself up on the pier. The pier needed work. It wouldn't last another year. Maybe

Todd ... but no, I knew I wouldn't be asking Todd for anything but a divorce. I'd been fooling myself for far too long.

I sat for a long time, soaking up the calm beauty, listening to the pine trees whisper their secrets, and letting the sun dry my clothes. I felt so tired, so old.

The low bass of Jason's stereo still beat dimly in the distance, but I simply didn't care. I headed back to the cabin and into our bedroom, changed into shorts and a tee shirt, and slipped under the yellow chenille bedspread. Sunlight streamed in the open window and dappled the pale walls. It danced and swayed and soon I fell asleep. Maybe if I hadn't, things would have been different. I don't know.

A loud, sharp sound woke me. I heard screaming and bolted out of bed. Dim, late-afternoon light streamed through the kitchen window, and I heard the rush of footsteps on the stairs. The door burst open and for a moment the silhouette of a stranger filled the doorway.

Then Todd stepped into the kitchen. His jeans and the front of his shirt were dark and wet. It took a second for my sleepy mind to realize he was covered in blood.

"My God, Todd! Are you hurt?" I took a step toward him, and then I saw the blood-spattered pistol in his hand.

"What are you doing with a gun?" Hysteria knocked along the edges of my brain.

Todd looked at his hand and seemed surprised the find the gun there. He dropped it as if it suddenly turned molten hot. The pistol fell in slow motion, cartwheeling through the air. It seemed to fall forever before landing with a "clunk" on the green linoleum. I expected it to fire, but it didn't.

Todd stumbled to one of the kitchen chairs and collapsed.

"It was an accident. I ... I didn't mean to," he stammered, covering his face with his bloody hands. "It was an accident."

Outside, a low, keening wail began. My legs felt boneless as I walked to the doorway. Mark was sitting on the bottom step sobbing and rocking.

"What happened?" I shook him, but he just kept moaning.

The Camaro's trunk was open. Shaking, I edged toward the back of the car. A small aluminum table was wedged against the back bumper. Glass dishes and metal pots were scattered on the ground. A propane tank sat on the table connected to a portable stove.

I knew enough to figure out it was some sort of drug lab, and then I wasn't afraid anymore. I was furiously angry again.

How could I have been so stupid? Drugs. It explained everything, Todd's erratic behavior, his inability to keep a job, the sudden friendship with Jason—everything fell into place. I was just missing one piece of the puzzle. Where was Jason?

A Redwing boot lay in the grass on the far side of the table. Heart thumping, I forced myself to walk around to the other side of the car. Jason's body was sprawled face-down in the grass. He lay still in a huge pool of blood. You didn't have to be a coroner to know he was dead. No one could lose that much blood and still be alive. A gaping wound made it look as if something exploded out the back of his body.

A green bottlenose fly buzzed, then landed in the bloody mess. It was too much. Black spots danced in front of my eyes, and I bit my lip to stay upright. I sat down hard in the grass, head between my knees, until the dizziness passed, and then I went to find Todd.

Mark had joined Todd at the table, and the two men, faces pale in the golden light of the kitchen, sat across from each other, passing an open whiskey bottle between them.

I found a Flintstone jelly glass in the cupboard, poured two fingers of whiskey, and drank it quickly.

"Yabba, dabba, doo," I toasted as the whiskey burned a trail of fire down my throat.

Raw whiskey on an empty stomach had quite a soothing effect, and both Todd and Mark were calm now, too.

"What happened?"

"I shot him, that's what happened." Todd said it matter-of-factly.

I remembered the gun. It was still on the floor, cold and malevolent.

"Okay, start from the beginning and tell me everything."

He did. He told me about his drug problem, about Jason's plan to make some "real money." He explained how the cabin was the perfect place to "cook some meth," isolated as it was, but something happened. Jason had gone crazy, accusing Todd of trying to rip him off.

"He got mad and came at me, so I hit him," Todd said. "That's when he reached into the trunk and pulled out the pistol. We wrestled over the gun, and it went off."

That was the shot I heard, the shot that ended Jason Warner's pathetic life, the shot that ended all our lives.

"We have to call the sheriff, Todd. Let me have the cell phone, and I'll drive out until I can get a signal."

"No, I don't think so, Kay." Todd said it quietly, but there was steel in his voice.

"Todd, we can't just..." I began.

"Shhh," he whispered, pressing his fingers against my lips. I tasted blood.

Todd poured me another drink and my hands shook as I picked up the whiskey and gulped it down.

"Kay, be reasonable. How would it look, the drugs and all? Do you think the local sheriff is just going to waltz up here, take one look around, and say, 'Don't worry, folks. These things happen.' Do you really see it playing out that way?"

"I don't know."

"Well, I do. Kay, you're in this, too. No one is going to believe you didn't know what was going on here. You're in it up to your neck, the same as us."

"But Todd, I didn't..." I started.

"But they don't know that, do they?"

"You could tell them I didn't have anything to do with it, the drugs or the other!"

"Why would they believe me?" Todd's face was dark and wolfish as the last rays of daylight fled the kitchen. "Face it, Kay, you're in this just as deep as me."

That was the moment everything changed. I believed Todd. I knew what Jason and Mark were, or I should have. I could have left the cabin, driven the Jeep back home when they showed up, but I didn't. I stayed. True, I didn't know anything about the drugs, but who would believe me? I'd like to think the whiskey played a part in my decision, but honestly, I don't know.

Mark broke the silence. "Man, I can't be around this. I'm on probation. I ... I can't be here!" He was becoming hysterical.

"Snap out of it, damn it!" Todd shouted. "You're in this, too. You want to go to prison? I sure as hell don't. Use your head, Mark!"

"What do we do?" Mark whispered, wiping tears away with his palms.

"We think, that's what we do."

Thoughts whirled around my head like angry gnats. Get rid of Jason and all our problems were solved. It was all Jason's fault anyway. He brought it on himself, bringing drugs and a gun to this pristine place. No one would miss him.

I thought about the conversation I'd overheard so many years ago. "You make your choices..." I heard my mother say. Yes, you make choices and then you live with them.

"I have an idea." I couldn't believe it was my voice outlining a plan to hide Jason's body, a plan to make it all go away. It was simple, really—the quarry. It was deep enough to hide Jason's car, the drug paraphernalia, and of course, Jason himself.

"Great, Kay, that's a great idea!" I could hear the pride in my husband's voice, but it didn't make me happy.

"We need to get rid of everything, especially that gun," I told them, downing another whiskey.

Todd picked up the pistol. He studied it for a long time then he looked at me. "Babe, you look pale. You alright?"

My stomach lurched. Staggering, I barely made it to the bathroom. I threw up. Then, head spinning, I crawled into the bedroom and passed out.

I woke up just before sunrise. The sky was a pale, shimmering purple. A loon cried out from somewhere on the lake. Todd sat on the edge of the bed smoking a cigarette.

"Todd..." my head pounded and my mouth felt dry and cottony. "Todd, we've got to go to the police. We've got to make this right."

"Babe, there's nothing left to make right. It's all taken care of. Everything's gone. Mark helped, and we took care of it last night, just like you said. The car, Jason, our clothes, everything's in the quarry. It worked like a charm, and no one will ever know."

But that wasn't the truth. I knew. He knew. And Mark knew.

"Babe, I'm so sorry this happened." Todd caught my hand and lifted it to his face. A slow tear rolled down his cheek. "I never meant any of it. I never wanted anything to come between us. Please forgive me. Please don't leave me. I love you."

For a moment, the man I married was there. This was the Todd I loved, vulnerable and sweet. I felt a rush of affection, a feeling I hadn't known for a long time. I knew then I could be strong. We'd get through this somehow. Todd held me and we made love, comforting each other as the world came awake.

Mark stayed at the cabin. He had to. He didn't have a ride back to the city. Todd and I tried to act as normal as possible, but Mark was having trouble. He spent his time in the other bedroom, hardly eating. At night, I heard him sob. If Todd noticed, he didn't mention it.

I avoided the backyard as long as I could, but on Thursday, I took some trash out to the burn pit. As soon as I stepped outside, I saw the blood. It looked like someone had gutted a deer in the driveway.

"Todd! Mark!" I yelled, "Get out here!"

They raced outside. Mark's face turned ashen.

"Jesus," he said.

"Deal with it!" I snarled at them.

They worked together cleaning up what I hoped was the only evidence left of Jason's death. I was washing dishes when a movement outside caught my eye. Mark knelt in the yard, using a small hand shovel to turn over the dirt. Todd eased up behind him. He was acting so strangely. I opened my mouth to call out, but before I could form the words, Todd lifted his arm. In his hand was the gun, the pistol that was supposed to be at the bottom of the quarry. There was a loud "pop" and Mark slumped forward in the grass.

Why didn't I leave? I couldn't say.

Todd buried Mark's body under the well house behind the cabin. I know, because I held the flashlight while Todd dug the grave.

"Why, Todd? Why?" I asked, finally.

"Babe, he was cracking up. Couldn't you hear him crying at night? He would have talked. You know he would."

He smiled at me, tamping down the last of the dirt. "It's for the best, really. This way only you and I know what happened. No one knew they were coming up here, not even you. We'll head home tomorrow and forget all about this. I love you, babe."

Todd looked at me and it felt like he was looking into my soul. "I did it for you, babe."

I couldn't meet his eyes, the eyes of a stranger. Heart thudding, I turned away.

"Why did you keep the gun, Todd? Why didn't you bury it with Mark? Why didn't you throw it in the quarry?"

"I didn't think about it," he said, his voice strained. "Don't worry. I'll stop by the quarry on the way out of here tomorrow. Kay, I'll take care of everything, you'll see."

That night, listening to Todd's steady breathing, I asked myself, "How could this have happened?"

Jason's death might have been an accident, but Mark? Mark was murdered. I saw it, standing in the kitchen with the buzz of cicadas in my ears, yet I did nothing. His blood was on my hands, too.

As I lay there, sleepless, I knew what had to be done. Soon as I could, I would call the police and tell them everything. I expect Todd knew that, too. Why else would he have kept the gun?

When I woke up, I was alone. The Jeep was in the driveway and the coffee was still hot, but Todd was nowhere around. I didn't look for him. Instead, I cleaned up the dishes he left in the sink and straightened up the bedroom.

In the drawer of the nightstand I found a pen and a yellowed tablet with the scores from a game of rummy on the first page. Carole won that game. Dust motes sailed on sunbeams and the room was eerily quiet as I sat on the edge of the bed studying the paper. I flipped the page, found the next clean one, and began to write. I wrote down everything that happened. My hands shook and I cried through most of it, but I got it all down on paper. I folded it and hid it inside my purse.

I was calm then. I knew our lives were over, but I also knew right from wrong. Like my mama said, you make your choices.

Slowly, I walked down the path to the lake. The pines on the far shore reflected in the water's mirror. The sun warmed them, and the air smelled of pine sap.

A kingfisher dove and caught a small fish. The dock wobbled, and I didn't have to turn around to know who was behind me. I waited. Would Todd put his arms around me or would gunfire be the last sound I heard?

Todd's reflection on the water answered my question.

"I'm sorry," Todd said, raising the gun to my head.

When I woke up, I was on a gurney. My head ached. The steady thrum of a helicopter sounded in the distance. I felt faint, and then I felt nothing.

The next time I awoke, I was in the hospital. Over the next few days, I learned that a backpacker camping illegally near the quarry heard Jason's car hit the water. He saw a white Jeep drive away, and when he hiked out, he notified the authorities.

With no radio or television at the cabin, we had no idea Jason's car had been discovered. The area was searched and from the tire tracks leading away from the quarry, law enforcement officials determined the direction the Jeep headed. A few days later, a conservation officer remembered the cabin. He and his partner decided to check it out.

They found the Jeep, and as they came upon us, they discovered Todd walking toward the lake with the gun in his hand.

I was lucky, very lucky.

As I stood watching the water and waiting, silver minnows darted through the sunlight under the dock. Water gently lapped the shore. A honeybee, yellow with pollen, flew by, and in that moment, I knew I was going to die. I was ready.

The gun clicked when he pulled the trigger. Nothing happened. I whirled around and looked Todd in the eye. His face was red and contorted. In one motion, he flipped the gun and swung it around, using it like a hammer. It hit me in the temple, and I went down like a rock.

The conservation officers burst through the trees, and Todd ran. One of the officers chased him while the other pulled me from the water. Todd made it to the Jeep and flew down the lane, but the tree-lined drive and the officers' truck blocked him in. The same gun that misfired and saved my life took my husband's.

The letter I wrote that morning went a long way to keeping me out of prison. A grand jury was convened, and again, I was lucky.

The cabin is up for sale. I have no desire to see it again. I visit it enough in my dreams. Mostly, it is Todd I see, bloodied and holding the gun. Sometimes he's a shadow, but I clearly see the gun he raises to shoot me. Lately, the teenagers lost so many years ago haunt my dreams.

I thought those ghosts had been laid to rest, but when divers were investigating Jason's car in the quarry, they discovered a cave. Inside the cave rested the bodies of those two young men. The cold water preserved them remarkably well.

We all make choices. We make our choices, then we live with them.

Poetry

Beth Anne
DeVonna Allison

With your old-fashioned name
your new-age heart calls you
to teach your keen students. In
an alien land where bombs are
walked into marketplaces
strapped to the chests of deluded
souls, you embody what is
worthy and decent about humanity,
a noble presence in an ignoble place.

When I wrote this poem in 2015, my friend Beth Anne Heesen was teaching English in a private school in Turkey, near a center of ISIS activity.

That Night upon the Moors
Monica Clark

The moon shone silver in the night,
the fairies danced in sheathes of light,
I never will forget the sight,
that night upon the moors.
With cold dew gleaming on the fern,
the heather dripped, and elf-flame burned,
I stood, and my heart swelled and yearned,
that night upon the moors.

A host of sprites, the Fairy Queen,
sparkled, soared in graceful sheens
of iridescent forest green,
that night upon the moors.

With wondrous drops of magic dew,
in golden orbs, the night wisps flew,
complete and utter joy, I knew,
that night upon the moors.

Then suddenly they disappeared,
and loneliness like fire seared,
bereft, I stood with flowing tears,
that night upon the moors.

Walking at Dawn on a Foggy Day
Monica Clark

Fog was draped like somber crepe upon the land as I crept by.
Cornstalk soldiers' bayonets pierced cold November sky.
I ambled through the lonely wood, a cozy, muffled lair,
Crow-black, withered branches, boney-fingered, combed the air.

Fog slithered low along the ground, a dank and murky tide
Soft and wet, it rolled and roiled, encased the countryside.
Timid gray-clad tendrils crawled along the river-lands.
Slow forays into twilight's gloom; invading, swirling bands.

Ol' Sol. that weary general, rode hard in from the east,
Fire-clad and battle-red, astride his fiery beast.
A bitter battle waged between two ancient, angry foes.
A draw at first 'til autumn-Zephyr winds began to blow.

The fog withdrew to fight again another misting day.
Upon the general's golden brow the crown of victory lay.

*Winner of the August 2006 Dana Literary Award

Whose Woods?
Monica Clark

Whose woods these are? Indeed, they're mine!
hough trespassed in from time to time
by poets, paupers, beggars, thieves,
who seek out answers they believe,
are hidden in diverging roads,
and what I do is chide and scold,
escort them to the road again,
and call the Law if they complain.

Last winter someone came at night,
with horse and sleigh, parked out of sight.
Seeking what? I've not a clue.
He must have been just passing through.
What draws these dreamers to my wood?
I find the places they have stood,
yet all I see are trees and brush,
I do not ken unearthly hush,
or understand epiphanies,
they seem to glean from rocks and trees.
Perhaps someday I'll understand,
for now, I chase them from my land.

Time, Like Frost
Monica Clark

Time, like frost,
paints trees and moss
the same translucent shade.
Between the lofty
and the low,
distinction is not made.

Garden Toad
Monica Clark

A toad, although a frog,
is not a sleek and handsome critter.
Instead, he's rather warty
and a craggy garden-sitter,
who dines on worms and insects,
and is very often seen;
he's that short and squatty fellow,
busy trundling through the beans.

The toad, he trills his toad-song
as he hunkers in the soil,
the Keeper of the Garden
who enjoys and loves his toil.
As he guards the rows of onions,
he is neither shy nor coy,
when it comes to garden helpers,
it's the toad whose most employed.

Hummingbird
Monica Clark

Hummingbird,
skittering, darting, humming,
hovering near each bloom he sees,
opulent, bold,
and iridescent,
sipping up gold,
cavorting with bees.

Poker Troubles
Monica Clark

My father took me hunting,
but we couldn't catch a deer.
So, he taught me how to gamble
over chips and ginger beer.

I learned the game of poker,
stud and draw and Texas hold 'em
Dad taught me how to ante,
what to bet, and when to fold 'em.

And when the trip was over
I taught all my friends to play.
We played cards at lunch and recess,
we played poker every day.

But what I didn't realize,
and my dad forgot to mention,
is that gambling in the classroom
earns a seven-day suspension.

So, I'm grounded 'til November
and my mom is pretty sad,
I can tell she's disappointed,
but she's really mad at Dad.

Dad is sleeping on the sofa.
Mom's been talking to our preacher.
And me? I'm pretty happy,
I won ten bucks from my teacher.

Night Visitor
Monica Clark

At ten 'til twelve, the child's face,
angelic, wrapped in sleep's embrace
while underneath her pillow hides
a precious pearl with ragged sides.

A figure slips inside the room,
hesitant in nightfall's gloom,
she's unadorned by gilded wings,
or pixie-dust and magic rings.

She finds the prize, she's quick and deft,
and carefully a dollar's left.
Another child's illusions fed,
the "Tooth Fairy" heads back to bed.

Abstract
Shanda Blue Easterday

As if apart from concrete existence
the molting, gray-white signets moved on the
bluest water, not applied or practical,
curious about the fisherman
on the pier, theoretical, abstruse
to them but not to their swan parents,
without reference to a specific instance
they raised their wings in a feathery clatter
depending on intrinsic form to warn
their young against humans as not so much
academic or hypothetical,
more removed, apart from feathered creatures
in their summation, condensation
of knowledge of dock-sitting fisher folk
and their preoccupied hooks, lost in thought.

Chloasma
Shanda Blue Easterday

The mask that exposes, does not hide
the face but reveals a woman as gravid,
pregnancy undisguised. Unlike Halloween
or a masked ball, more like a pattern
of characters, bits or bytes to control
elimination or retention
of another, maybe underlying
pattern of characters, bits or bytes,
this tan border framing the face like
the translucent space surrounding
a television picture tube or screen,
this melasma is not that opaque
margin placed between a source of light
and a photo-sensitive surface
preventing its exposure, its imprinting
but more symbolic or symptomatic,
exposing the underlying condition.

Cleave
Shanda Blue Easterday

Because a hoof may not be cloven, a sign
of the devil, to cleave seems desperate,
a severance too harsh to be the key, clef,
clovis, yet related, distant cousins
from a split ovum generations passed
the way a key creates an opening
makes a space, a way through, a doorway,
yet the way a rusty key fits a
corroded lock not wanting to move but
to stick fast, adhere, become attached, cleave.

Feet
Shanda Blue Easterday

I tell her to knit stockings or slippers,
so practical, because women are not
allowed to paint or even draw the body
or parts of the body nor allude to
the body except in the most oblique
terms. So, make some stockings, I say, but she
says knitting is too usefully tedious
with those tiny needles and hundreds of
miniature stitches, carefully counted
ribbed ankles, tiresome turned heels and toes.
It's so trying to make so little progress
after hours of clicking stitches in a
stuffy parlor. She prefers charcoal's thick,
quick dark line and that swath of water-color
from the brush, the object revealed
in moments, not hours, in colors, not
simple white or black thin cotton or wool
merino careful stockinette stitches.

Cucurbita pepo
Shanda Blue Easterday

Her garden planted with corn to support
beans, legumes to shade squash, summer askuta
squash, a thing to be eaten raw, in the front
rows, *cucurbita pepo*, pumpkin squash
in the back rows for autumn and winter
pies, pepitas, flat, dark green, treats dried
and roasted to keep winter months well fed,
Sarah rises in the dew of an early
August morning, the project, pumpkin
pollination. Noting few neighborhood
bees, she dons garden clogs, long pants, long sleeves,
treks through over-large leaves on over-long vines
to investigate blossom gender, to
finger the male for its pollen, carry
golden dust to the other, ovary
bearing blooms, this pollinator of winter
food, warmth, and dreams.

Floor
Shanda Blue Easterday

Viewed through the gallery window, she stood,
the floor supported her and the glass case
or counter behind which she used the fingernail
of her right index finger to push back
the cuticles of her left fingers, her gaze
met that of the darkly suited man looking
from a car stopped at the traffic signal.
He was not stunned but she was overwhelmed
and turned her eyes down to her tablet lying
on the glass counter top, feeling herself
transparent when she preferred opacity,
she tried to think of a forest floor,
imagine trees to avoid watching
the auto leave the intersection, flowing
around the corner like a small school
of fish skirting a coral pile on the
ocean bottom. He was no big fish on
the floor of this assembly, this meant-to-be-
short relationship. Neither was he a tree
felled silently and lying on the ground
in this metaphysical wood. She turned
her attention back to the business of
this building in which she stood, was not knocked
down on its ground level, its nadir.

Leash Slipped
Shanda Blue Easterday

On her way to breakfast out Thursday
morning, when folks in town for a funeral,
and the regulars are eating bacon,
eggs, toast, in the little corner café,
she's passed by a truck pulling an almost
windowless trailer emblazoned "Cottage,"
but even ancient cottages have more
windows than this white box on wheels.

She seats herself, as the sign suggests, in
a usual booth where her husband sits
with her on Sunday mornings, early,
before church; the waitress pours her coffee,
gives her a conspiratorial look,
alone in a restaurant, in a small town,
leash slipped.

Matter
Shanda Blue Easterday

What matters occupies space, perceived by
the senses, has physical substance
even in the universe, has mass, exists
solid, liquid, or gas, a specific
type. What matters includes the substance
of thought or expression, subject of concern
or action, is trouble or difficulty,
an approximated quantity or
something of importance, printed or written
as any art can be concrete or non-
concrete, ephemeral, inorganic
matter or anti-matter, opposite
charge and magnetism. Writing this
is another way of being not what
society wants but what society
doesn't want, the poet. Crossing to safe-
ty, yellow is wide, contrary. Must creation be conscious? A new lens has been
invented for the big screen, big picture:
Chicago for New York in any light.

Trying Not to Think
Shanda Blue Easterday

The swans are a puzzle who stay for winter
on our little lake. They have great capable,
clattering wings but don't fly south, or only
fly as far south as the end of the lake where
it empties into feisty Fawn River, that
sometimes stony rapid water. For exercise,
or perhaps a wintery outing, the swans fly
up to our end, circle, turning 'round over
the boat launch, deserted in snowy ice, cold days;
evenings they settle, paddle some small darkling
blue water spot open. They are tough, beautiful
as women, protective, weathering winter.

Inspired by the 2016 presidential election and the Women's March

Reading by Candlelight
Hedy Habra

Bent over the page, I watch the light of the candle cast fluid shadows,
the way the cypress pierces low clouds with its vertical green flame,
flaring will-o'-wisps spring from the spiral staircase of my consciousness,
ferns unfurl in slow motion, spread liquid color at dawn
as fronds fill spaces once covered with snow,
the hearth's fiery tongues my cat and I watch flicker all night long,
the blue flame rising when I'd flambé cognac over crêpes suzettes,
the flicker of a match lighting a cigarette,
the infamous flames of a pyre or an auto da fe in a central square,
the flame of a candle I read about, lighting Camoens' table,
his cat sitting on a pile of notes eyes gleaming at the waning wick,
the poet keeps writing in the dark under the light shed from the eyes of his cat,
the tall flames casting a shadow-show of a couple's encounter over the walls of a cave,
flames rising from Beirut at night, as we watched from the mountains during the civil war
the flames of violence filtered by the TV screen, more virtual each day, still color the news, images hiding the smell of blood and charred skin.

First published by *Sequestrum*

After the Storm
Hedy Habra

Dead trees erect as Dali's crutches,
hold broken branches in angled joints,
forsaken trophies no one reclaims, tangled
in old vines, disjointed, distorted bones,

elephant skin filled with memories
I wish to rip, fragment, discard as I pull,
uproot trees still resisting, conjuring
up new shoots, refusing to give up.

I gather strewn twigs like an automaton
in an open-air ossuary revealing desecrated
fossils flown from thickets and tall branches,
pile them up at the farthest end of the creek,

throw them away with all my strength,
watch the arc they form in the air,
see how they land on the other side
in a cemetery of lost illusions.

I reach for a hanging branch with blue patina,
a sunken treasure the color of my dreams,
its hollow, brittle limbs easy to break,
tsik...tsik, one by one, tsik...tsik...tsik...

Grit and Grace

Others, I leave on the side of the paths,
sculptures too heavy to lift, nature's
Petri dishes, grounds for rippled
mushrooms writing their own memoir
in the hidden calligraphy of their folds.

First published by *Danse Macabre*
From *Under Brushstrokes* (Press 53 2015)

Tea at Chez Paul's
Hedy Habra

We ate Schtengels at *Chez Paul's*,
twisted breads sprinkled with coarse salt
clinging to our lips.
We could see the sea enfolding us
through the tall bay windows
of the semi-circular Swiss teahouse.
You described a Phoenician Tale
just for me,
how the mountain slopes
reddened each spring
with Adonis' blood,
how this delicate flower,
truly and duly Lebanese
has come to be called a red poppy, an anemone,
with all its melodious variations,
alkhushkhash,
un amapola,
un coquelicot,
ed anche un papavero...

We walked through a field scattered
with red poppies bright as when Ishtar
sprinkled nectar
on her beloved's blood.
Time seemed elastic then,
space infinite.
I wished to bring home a handful of scarlet light,

to keep the softness of its wrinkled petals
alive a while longer.
The moment I cut Adonis' flower,
hanging like a broken limb, its corolla fell over my hand,
head too heavy with dreams.
No wonder blossoms tremble
on their fragile stem.

Sometimes love is only real when not uprooted.
Isn't there a geography of every emotion?
not a precious, intricate *Carte du Tendre*,
but a trail of forgotten footsteps mapping
every heartbeat, every motion?
A stairwell, a car, a booth, a parking lot,
a streetlight, a gateway,
an old-fashioned reverbère,
a bus stop or maybe a tree, a tree stump,
a moss-covered path, a pond,
a small creek, a flat stone,
a hill, a porch or even a wooden bench?

Take the poppy, for instance. It will only breathe
and give joy at its birthplace.
I can still feel the small flower melting
into liquid silk in my palm.
I held the red petals to my cheek
like a morning kiss while you kept telling how Ishtar
or as some may say Astarté, often mistaken for Isis,
was truly her Phoenician incarnation,
before she was ever called Aphrodite or Venus.
I remember how you talked and talked
until we both stepped into Ishtar's temple.

First published by *Nimrod International Journal,* Pablo Neruda Award Finalist
From *Tea in Heliopolis* (Press 53 2013)

Blue Heron
Hedy Habra

An Egyptian sculpture
lost in the Northern wilderness,
the blue heron stands out
in the whitened landscape,
mimics an ibis' fixed stare,
studies the frozen creek,
sensing trembling gills
beneath the transparent sheet.

But why land in my backyard,
I wonder, where no lotus ever grows?
Unless he sees his own ancestral roots
in my wide-open eyes lined with kohl,
and knows that water from the Nile
still runs in my veins since birth.

In warmer seasons he has seen me
feed the silver fish,
tend the vegetable garden,
bend over perennials
springing stronger each year,
add more seeds,
making this our home,
where we've lived the longest ever.

Today he saw me walk in circles
in the stillness of barren trees
over crisp snowflakes
masking all signs of life,
the forget-me-nots throbbing
under their icy coat, scintillating,

a thousand suns
opening a dam of flowing memories
on sunnier shores
promises of blossoms to come

until suddenly, as if pulsated by an engine,
statuesque, the migrant bird deploys gigantic
wings, disappears through the dead branches.

First published in *Come Together: Imagine Peace*
From *Tea in Heliopolis* (Press 53 2013)

Open-Air Cinema in Heliopolis
Hedy Habra

You used to say, mother:
"Let me see your face when lit
by a crescent moon:
every day of the month
will smile the way you do."

We saw double-feature movies
in open-air theatres.
The cool breeze ran through our hair,

over our necks, lifted our skirts,
swayed us in a magical carpet.

Tempted by vendors chanting
Greek cheese and sesame breads,
we often stayed, sipping icy lemon
granitas through replays, the lift
and pause of cascading light.

Characters entered our own
camera obscura.
We never agreed on their age:
you added a few years,
I wanted them closer to mine.

I remember a recurrent scene,
fading now into a sepia cameo,
where a woman—always the same
yet different—slaps a man
before falling in his arms.

I watched your face then,
as stars outlined the sky,
the slight opening of the lips,
the Gioconda's elegant smile
you allowed yourself,
befitting the sfumato of the late hours.

Arm in arm, we walked home,
following the trail of the moon.

First published by *Cutthroat: A Journal of the Arts*, Pablo Neruda Award Finalist
From *Tea in Heliopolis* (Press 53 2013)

A Pantoum in Flight
Ingrid Lochamire

If I feed them, for certain they will come,
Feathered fellows, fleet on furling wing,
They'll flock and flit to peck and gather some
Seed, perchance their native song to sing.

Feathered fellows, so fleet on furling wing,
Sit peering through glass while they grow full
On seed, perchance their native song to sing.
Do they care who gave them nut and hull?

Peering through glass, they flee once they grow full,
Streaks of red, blue, brown against the sun.
But do they care? Who gave them nut and hull?
Feed them again. I'm certain they will come.

Fairy Tale
Kathleen McGookey

Offer me a peach and a fork. Offer my sadness a small box. Red or gold or white, it doesn't matter. Please don't touch the lit candles on the tree. Store the box until I want it, then tell me a story, the one where I'm happy as a trout because no one catches me. The trout wants a box to call its own. The red fox wants to swim across the river. The bear ran away from the woodsman, then fell asleep in the honey tree. If only we had a brand new axe! Open my box, and you'll find my brand-new child. I've been wanting the two of you to meet.

Originally appeared in *The Literary Review*.

Pain Lake
Kathleen McGookey

Dive in, leave yours behind. Or just dip your toe. Afterward, you can sit and watch the sky bleed. Someone will hand you a dandelion bouquet and a glass of water. Someone will braid your hair. The wooden sign by the water is faded now. If the wind kicks up, you can chase beach balls with the kids and dogs who splash by the reeds. Yes, they feel it. More than you'd think. It is unfortunate or not, depending.

Originally appeared in *Great River Review*.

Lighthouse Tour, South Manitou Island
Kathleen McGookey

Lake Michigan heaves its slow heartbeat on the sand. The tower narrows the higher we go. My son stomps on each lattice metal step and sand from his shoes sifts through. The tour guide stops our group on each progressively smaller landing, asks, *What part of this lighthouse was built first?* and, after we've climbed through a trapdoor that disappears into floor, *What happened in this room?* I don't lean in or look down. My daughter tugs her braids and asks for my camera. The guide offers a story: here, two older brothers watched their parents' boat go down in a storm. A little light, extinguished, while the lighthouse blinked *I'm here*. At the top, we are allowed outside. *It'll be windy*, the guide says, *so take off your hats*. I glimpse a thin railing and reach for my children. *If you drop anything*, the guide says, *just let it fall*.

Originally appeared in the *Dunes Review*.

Red Ants, Black Ants
Adella Najaro

An ant crawling through tattered books and files
hid under the shelf until I pinched it within
a thin white tissue. It didn't have wings, but
it could have been a termite preparing to bore
into wallboard and chew its way down
to the foundation. How strange

the way one ant on a wall next to a nail
comes forth unknown. A harbinger of why
I hate black ants and why Abuelita preserved
the red ones in mason jars. I have trouble
mixing the Wild West with Managua, Nicaragua,
1908. Managua had to be green, but the poverty

and isolation of dry desert mesquite, beans
bubbling in an iron pot, fit stories
of hunger. Everyone. My grandmother stole
into the kitchen wearing a white
cotton frock embroidered with pineapples.
It could have been pale blue or yellow.

Definitely sleeveless in that humidity
and heat. Clear night skies are not frozen cold,
but a time when aunts, uncles, cousins and
grandmothers dream without sound.
Iguanas and monkeys. Huge cockroaches
with wings. In the night, a crescent moon would

have been enough for her to reach into a box lined
with wax paper. An iron box. A spicy hunk
of meat in her little scavenging hands
and the ants. The red ants biting her tongue.
Why do we love our families so much?
I had a hammer and nails. A piece of plywood.

I was determined to pound straight and true
under a Los Angeles sun and Abuelita's tomatoes,
five pearly bushes six feet tall. Green in arid
desert heat. From the garden hose, water
came out hot and splashed to dry dust. I sat
on clumps of grass, the board between my legs.

The nails wouldn't stay straight! They flopped
over as the hammer hit the head. It was hot.
I was sweaty, dirty and crying. Those damn
nails! And the ants crawling on my sneakers,
in my sock, up my leg! I'm sure she came out
and wiped me off; had me blow my nose

and gave me a piece of pie. It wasn't pie.
It was *torta*. Out of a mix, but changed. An extra
egg. Whole milk. Los Angeles. Managua.
Verdant green mangroves and tile roofs.

Cleaning House
Adela Najarro

And it is a lie if I tell you that I am any different.
In my mother's house there are multiple uses

for strange glass jars and doll-sized iron kettles.
The universe is not organized and set

but instead fluctuates in a chaotic dance
orchestrated by stashing into boxes

photos that are never to be labeled or sorted.
It is true she is not a very good housekeeper

and cleaning has always been impetuous
and without particular reason. A mystery

of not knowing why or when papers get lost
and keys misplaced, a nod to gnomes and gremlins,

half of the expected whole. The coldness of life
is what always happens. My mother's

dead father was laid out on a table, neatly
tucked and folded into a lightweight suit.

She reached out to one yellow calcified toe, a fleeting
touch. If only I could accept the falling away

of my own father, perhaps I would be granted white
blossoms and green fronds growing up and out

from moisture and soil, granted to me what
my mother saw and holds in her heart: it's just

the way the world is. Chaos. Disorder.
That which does not hold still. We each try

to do what we can: dust, cook,
love without grand conclusions.

If only to believe it all works
together, that water in a pond

reflects an accurate image,
that we can trust

what is here and now.

Near Traverse City, Michigan
Adela Najarro

In the distance, a sand dune ladled out by storm. It looks
like a bear lumbering through grass, thistle, and piping clover.
There is a view station and pale pine fencing. The trail

down is long and steep. Standing above turquoise blue
water, I think of my toes on a diving board
and a somersault into a swimming pool in San Francisco.

The fact that my chubby little hands reached around
thick thighs and dimpled knees for a quick twirl mid-air
had been a true acrobatic feat. The fat girl was free

from the bounds of gravity. That's what I was: the fat girl
displacing water onto cement and tile. My father's wife
noted the poor state of affairs I was forced to live in:

too many Hostess Fruit Pies and Twinkies. But I know
how to wait for flowers undulating toward a light house
where no one lives anymore. Near Traverse City,

fields roll through cables blasted into wood and tree limbs
flare fire over the roofs of barns. There is a hot-tub,
fill-line, and my impatience to sink into pulsating water

with a man who loves my belly curving down to his mouth.

The Swarming Background
Adela Najarro

When the snow melted, my cigarette butt
was on the lawn. This was before Steve fell

on his knees with a smile and apology for being
47 minutes late, a mocha in hand, as if coffee

would take him somewhere besides Boston where
he met Janine. A side of toast, butter and marmalade.

A spoon rinsed clean in the sink. I climbed into bed,
bumped into a suitcase, and birds began ending

the long quiet during which snow made white
air around seven windows of an old house cut up

into four one-bedroom apartments. Yes, I do count
moments as they pass Sycamore Avenue and bricks

interlaced down a hill. In 1856 wagon wheels
careened through mud. The soil dried, cracked,

and goldenrod burst as a bungee cord broke
while a man fell on the edge of an airbag the size

of St. Louis. We need a beginning and end to quell
an angel in a church graveyard. Black marble

Grit and Grace

wings on a postcard from Iowa, where I refused to go
sightseeing in a cemetery, but I saw a Jersey cow,

its long tongue on a salt lick. A woman needs water
after hands on a steering wheel and throwing change

at a toll booth. Mountains rise above a desert,
ocean, and highway. The 405 runs through

California where Cindy, Robin and I sat on grass
under a tree. We were ten. Nothing much happened.

San Francisco
Adela Najarro

My great-grandmother taught my mother to read using chalk
    and a black slate in León where adobe brick
        buildings are white-washed Spaniards

and history. We brought with us red and blue macaws, panthers,
    and crocodiles. Tooling up and down
        Dolores Street hills, my papi rode

a bicycle delivering Lela's nacatamales. Back and forth
    from a clock tower at the end of Market Street,
        a renovated 1919 streetcar,

transplanted from Milan, works tourist dollars. Advertisements
    from the late sixties posted behind
        True View Plexiglass. I can't read a word

of the Italian glitz, nor fathom the deep blue of the Mediterranean
    while sipping an ice cold Coca-Cola, but there is a
    warm blanket
        on a wooden bench and a leather

hand hook. Above a Cuban restaurant, where waiters serve
    black bean hummus and chocolate croissants,
        hangs the gay pride flag alongside

Grit and Grace

<pre>
a Direct TV satellite dish. Gabby walks to school, Pokémon
        cards in his pocket. Sanchez Street. I work
            in the kitchen with my Lela. Mariposa Avenue,

Valencia Street, Camino Real, are added to masa. Homemade
        tortillas puff into sweetness. I'm not
            one-third Irish, one-half German

and two parts English with a little Cherokee thrown in,
        but last night I couldn't translate the word "hinge"
            on every door that opens and closes

to clouds beyond four walls. An old lady, perhaps Cambodian,
        Vietnamese, Korean, something of her own,
            hurries off the 31 Stockton while

my Tía Teresa double parks in front of the mercados on
    24th Street
        para los quesos y los chiles in the backroom. One
            whiff and the world is not so small.
</pre>

Lauds
Donna Perkins Pierce

Wing flap, slap water, feet churn
Canada Geese rise above river fog
circle once, twice, individuals, pairs
scramble into place, a mighty skein
against orange sun.
Follow me,
honks back goose to goose,
echoes across the oxbow

My Teacher
Donna Perkins Pierce

My trainer,
my God,
how I long to follow you
faithfully, wholly
but I am like a wild colt.
Impatient with your pace,
I buck and twist.
Unsure of your path,
I break and run.
Then, you catch my halter
and start again.
Your discipline, guidance and
pure love
reign me in,
return me to you way.
With your hand
I walk, trot, gallop
turn right or left
back up and
stand still.
I learn to trust your lessons, trust you.
Today I know you are the god
of the mundane,
of the magnificent,
of the miraculous.

I will thank you
in the barn,
in the arena,
on the trails.

November Garden
Donna Perkins Pierce

Sun rays oblique,
frost patchy on dry grass,
plant stalks mostly withered, brown.
Brussel sprouts still green,
sugars concentrated by cold morning air.
I stoop, fill my basket, ponder how
standing against adversity can
bring out sweetness as well as strength.

Too Many Chickens Are Coming Home to Roost
Patricia Jabbeh Wesley

Let us open the doors. Let us lift the shutters
over the thresholds of the doors, let us
remove the bars from the door posts,
too many chickens are coming home to roost,

and it is not the storm. It is not August
September Hurricane. It is not the storm
that's driving home all the angry of heart,
all the hate that, like aged tar on broken

pavement, has lifted onto the roads, and now,
too many chickens are coming home to roost.
Let us open the doors, not to let them in.
Let us open the doors to let us out.

Do not turn down your lights. Do not go to
bed with your eyes closed. Do not let out your
young sons. Do not wander into unknown places.
Do not listen to the wind. Too many roosters

have come home to drive us away from town.
We who came running from the fires of our
homelands are now being told to flee again.
Too many roosters have come home to roost

Grit and Grace

because hate is not a thing we can hold
in a sift. Hate is not a thing we can place a finger
upon to soothe away hurt. Hate is as hard
as a burning stone, as hard as pain, as an open sore.

Copyright: Patricia Jabbeh Wesley and *Cutthroat, a Journal of the Arts, Truth to Power*, (Durango, CO, 2017)

Suburbia
Patricia Jabbeh Wesley

To each, their groundhog,
their slanting rolling hills, their green green
of endless lawns, and if a house
could bow, there it is, Pennsylvania.
And to each, their heavy SUVs
so the hills can climb higher
or the cars can navigate the hills
of snowy cliffs when winter
arrives, and the groundhog no longer
can bathe under the sun under my trees
under my brush under my under-deck
under my eyeballs under my nerves
where a backyard can scare
away buyers, fearful their toddler
may someday fall down my groundhog,
cliffs, where a herd of deer may walk freely
up these my cliffs without falling.

As if a toddler were a stand-alone thing,
unhooked to mother unlike a family of deer.
They want me to level the hills
to the level of leveled hills.
They want me to move the house,
to push, to push and push until
the house is pushed further onto
leveled ground where ground keeps its level.
They want me to level myself to the level

of ground, of brainless days of leveling
everything to the level of unleveled things.
They want this house at the level
of the groundhogs and squirrels
and the only surviving, passing deer.
They want me to level the cost
to the level of wild flowers, to bring
myself to the level of ground.
To each their worries of wealth,
their passing feet of not knowing
who the next-door neighbor is.

In Case of Water Landing
Patricia Jabbeh Wesley

To fly into Michigan, you must first fly over Michigan.
Wet, penetrating, surfing, unreliable as any lake can be.

Anything insoluble will demand another route.
At the outskirts of what looks like any city, Chicago

stands, defiant, edgy and biting. The heavy musky sky
with skyscrapers at the edge of a world on edge.

Passengers must sit stiff until land comes in sight,
after Chicago fades into sky and the lake recedes into

itself, Michigan emerges at last, a state, no longer
a body of water. I love the feeling of staying afloat,

but landing is such a good thing. The feet were made
to dwell on solid ground. Imagine Noah docking

on water after The Flood, leading hundreds of animals
afloat on a cushion from beneath his Ark's seat. But Noah

would not dock until he'd found land, knowing how
dependable only land is, something water is forever

seeking to know. On my flight, the attendant is teaching
us how to stay alive in a crash, how to stay afloat, how

to pull out the cushion from beneath our legs, our hands
holding on tightly to the air mask, the other hand, pulling

out the cushion. And if you are seated at the exit, you will
need a third hand to open the heavy metal door and lead

everyone onto air. The cushion will be good for water
landing, for the air bubbles that ride upon wet waves.

Just hang on to the cushion and the mask and then let go
of the seat belt because the plane is now jerking, crashing,

exploding, in search of water. Remember, the cushion is still
being held by your trembling other hand you never really had.

The cushion, she says, is great for floatation, a device
originally meant for floating during a plane crash until

someone placed it beneath your large bottom to float on
while the plane still floats on air. Any time one needs

a cushion to float on in case of water landing, it is
no landing at all. Have you ever seen a plane crash survivor

who landed on water and got out floating on a floatation
device from beneath an airplane's seat? I love the earth,

its cruel solidity of crushed surfaces, iron rocks, dust,
sand and muck. Trees do not have to make themselves felt

since they are always called trees. But I see, our plane
has crossed Lake Michigan into Michigan, at last.

Copyright: Patricia Jabbeh Wesley, *The River is Rising* (Autumn House Press, Pittsburgh, PA 2007)

Shakespeare 550
Patricia Jabbeh Wesley

Shakespeare stalks my basement corridors, in
between dusty pages, his long gray beard and tiny

spectacles, calling out to Hamlet to put away
the sword. Hamlet, who will not let Claudius alone.

My professor teaches Shakespeare the way
only Macbeth could have taught Shakespeare.

She weeps when she teaches King Lear and his
good-for-nothing daughters. King Lear, weeping

in the storm, King Lear giving away his fortune
before his death. My professor wipes her large,

blue eyes when she remembers King Lear.
I pity my professor who weeps for King Lear.

My professor who loves the storm and the rain
and King Lear, caught in the rain. She was

Shakespeare's lover when he wrote Macbeth,
the two of them, sitting beside the fireplace,

editing Macbeth. She loves Macbeth who plots
his own death at midnight, when the fireplace

is finally cold, and only witches can prowl dark
hallways while a dagger strikes home. My professor

envies Macbeth who stalks his own hallways
with a dagger. Macbeth who can kill his enemies

so easily. Everyone should be able to kill their enemies
with a dagger. Everyone should be able to wash their

hands clean at the end of a class. I am afraid of my
professor's eyes, her organized smile. After so long,

I can still see my professor standing under the oak tree
on my block, talking with the weeping king who

reminds her of her dead father and the snow
falling lightly outside. Her cold hands and feet,

her cold white tears. Today my professor killed
Shakespeare and Othello and Macbeth and Hamlet

and Ophelia, and all the huge books on my table.
Her own Othello with his brute face and hands.

Othello with an inflamed face, his foaming mouth.
Death is an angry God in Shakespeare, I'd say.

When my professor discusses Othello, students
sit mute, staring up at her telling us that Othello

is a brute pagan who murders Desdemona, his wife.
If he had killed a Moor like himself, it wouldn't

have been murder, she says. She wants to put Othello
to death, but Othello is already dead, like Macbeth,

like Hamlet and Claudius, all of them, dead, like
King Lear, like Shakespeare. I should have told her

to let Othello die, to let Shakespeare die the way
he massacred all those fine people. Shakespeare,

who knew how to murder with the sword.
Let the dead bury the dead, I should have said.

Copyright: Patricia Jabbeh Wesley, *The River is Rising* (Autumn House Press, Pittsburgh, PA 2007)

Poem Written from Failed Chat Notes
Patricia Jabbeh Wesley

"Hi PJ," someone writes, the PJ, calmer than
the owner of the name. I love to see my initials
so free of all the cares of earthly possessions.
"Looking for job," another writes, just like
that, looking for a job. The message is flat,
like a pan, no, no, like a flat board, where
the cutting of potatoes further flattens
the map where the job may be found.

"Hello," the echo, clearly discernible
through the pressing of keys, this time,
a woman, out there in Southeast Asia, "Hello,"
she says, as if words were sufficient
in themselves to return to us, filled
with air bubbles, like a balloon.

"Hello, madam," one man says like a sigh,
carrying the silence that only the word
"madam" can leave behind. I check him out,
and his hair, combed back as if after shower.
Somewhere in India, it is hot now.
"How r you today?" another adds,
as if to complete the sentence
others have left hanging
on the tiny lines of these long distance
greetings, like litter on the page of a phone.

"Hi, how r u?" another interjects, and as
quickly as that came in, here comes
another, in correction of grammar, I guess,
"How are u today?" So I think, we should
all agree that the proper spelling of "you"
has to be "u." But before I linger too long
on whether a "u" is better than "you,"
here comes another, more elaborate,
a lecture on the act of caring,
something I needed to hear today.
But when I do not respond, another comes
in, maybe to take back his long discourse,
he says, simply and calmly, "Hello."
I love the word better. "Hello." At least I can
write a poem with that. Hello, hello, imagine

a poem with a hundred hellos all over the
page, a hundred and fifty hellos.
When the next greeting stops at something
like, "Hello, big sis," I step away from
the computer to check my weight.
For a moment, I think he meant "big,
fat, overweight, large," what can I say
to another brother of mine far across
the ocean somewhere? I love Facebook's
ability to tie us through air and space
by hanging strings and names.

After a while, I'm tired of reading.
All across the message inbox are fragments
of disconnected thoughts unending,
the fracturing of thoughts by people who
could be otherwise, fractured. So, like

pieces of jumbled up thoughts, I read on
and on, "Patricia," "Hi," "Mm," "Hey,"
"Hello, mam," "Good morning," "hey,"
"Wat's up?" "Oh," "Mam," "What's up?"
In between the carefully incompleteness

of language, are those whose stories no one
will tell. I wish I knew the next sentence,
the twisting of a finger on a small keyboard
just to scribble a single word. Someday,
there will be strings of words strung together
so another can complete the thoughts of another.
I love you all, I say to myself, but most of all,
I love the incompleteness with which
you complete the things you cannot say.

Previously published in *Asian Signatures Literary Journal*, 2013, copyright, Patricia Jabbeh Wesley

Creative Non-Fiction

Of Sukkah and Muezzins
DeVonna R. Allison

My bed groaned comfortably as I turned, trying in vain to snatch a few more hours of sleep. An oscillating fan pushed stuffy air around the room and I reached for my phone. It was just 4:30 in the morning, local time. Doing the quick calculation in my head, I realized why I was not sleeping. My body clock was set to the American Eastern Standard Time zone where it was currently 11:00 am. But I was not at home. A thrill of excitement shot through me when I recalled, again, that I was in Ariel, an Israeli settlement in the Palestinian West Bank.

I threw the covers back carefully, so as not to disturb Beth Anne, my roommate, and crept onto the landing outside our bedroom. I closed the door softly. Immediately to my left were the stairs that led down to the main floor of the house. Across the hall, doors were closed to the bedrooms where my travel companions slept. I crossed to the right in the hall, ceramic tiles cool beneath my feet, and slid the glass door aside to exit the house and enter the balcony. Sliding the door closed behind me, I relaxed and breathed deeply in the pre-dawn coolness of the outdoors. I knew this fleeting hour was but a brief break from the day's heat.

Below the balcony in the yard was a small chicken house and a cluster of fruit trees carefully tended by the family that lived there.

Spread across the valley before from me were the hills of Samaria, dotted with distant Palestinian villages, dimly lit by sparse streetlights. The sky was dark above, the stars gleaming.

I stood at the cement rail of the balcony and drank in the sight. I wanted to savor the moment for I was realizing a dream—the dream to visit the ancient land of Israel. Behind me on the balcony was the family's sukkah, a temporary hut built outdoors by observant Jews and Christians during the time of the Feast of Tabernacles. The sukkah represented the forty years of wandering in the wilderness following the Israelite exodus from Egypt. Each sukkah was different; the unique creation of the family who made it. The top of this sukkah's metal frame was covered loosely with palm branches and its sides were draped with sheer fabric that was drawn back to allow a panoramic view of the hilly plains spread below. I entered the sukkah, lay down on a chaise and looked up through the scant ceiling. According to tradition, the roof was to be made so that the stars were visible at night. A light breeze disturbed the sheer material that made up the walls. Peace enveloped me, and also a unique joy that I'd only felt since my arrival days earlier; the joy of being present in this ancient land so dear to my faith.

My brief reverie was interrupted by a faint crackling sound that came to me, echoing through the darkness. This was followed by a man's voice, monotone yet lyrical.

"Allahu akbar, allahu akbar..." the voice intoned and I realized this was the adhan, the Muslim call to prayer. It was the first of five such calls that would issue forth that day and probably the one easiest to hear due to the clear quiet early morning.

Each Arab village scattered throughout the valley had its own mosque, their minaret towers visible for miles. I heard the crackling again and again, and yet again. Each crackle was the switching on of a speaker and was followed by another man's voice. The call to early-morning prayer was being issued by each mosque in the valley, individually instructing its own faithful to pray. Within minutes the sleeping valley was echoing with the adhan from every corner. Goosebumps crawled along my flesh as I sat up in the sukkah, listening to the voices until one by one they faded. I lay back in the sukkah again, heavy-eyed, yet still unable sleep. Now, however, it wasn't the time change that kept sleep at bay; it was the realization that I was in the Middle East.

Encounter
DeVonna R. Allison

An icy wind threaded its way through the deserted gas pumps as I struggled with the door to my gas tank. It was January in Michigan and the arctic air had frozen the tank's access door; I needed help. I looked around the empty station before noticing a man crossing the street in my direction.

Even from a distance I could see the man's stained coat was open to the wind that tossed his straggling hair and beard. I hesitated for a moment, but when that same wind set the ends of my scarf whipping straight out in front of me I called out to the stranger.

"Excuse me sir, could you help me, please?"

The man came over and when I'd explained my problem he agreed to help me. Standing as close as he was, I became aware the stranger was unwashed.

Showing him the release lever next to the driver's seat, I took my place at the tank's opening. Looking back, I noticed my wallet lying open on the driver's seat and mere inches away from the stranger's hand. My cash was plainly visible.

Better get this over with quickly, I determined; the sooner this stranger was on his way again, the more comfortable I'd feel.

I nodded to him, and while he pulled the lever I successfully pried the access door open with my credit card. I confess, now, that I was a little too relieved as I thanked him for his help. Now we could go our separate ways again.

But the stranger didn't leave. Instead, he stood motionless, silently looking at me. We were only a step apart and the chill traveling the length of my spine now had nothing to do with the weather.

"Thank you," he said. "Thank you for letting me help you." And turning, the stranger continued on his way, across the frozen parking lot, into an icy wind.

Field of Geese
DeVonna R. Allison

I rode through a field of wild geese today.

I arrived home from a demoralizing job interview, pulled up to the mailbox and removed the usual bills and an ominous-looking notice from the bank and shivered. The day was damp and chilly, matching my mood.

Up our driveway, at the house, I was greeted by the sight of my paint horse peering over his gate, ears forward, head up, wordlessly inviting me to spoil him. Geronimo was my guilty pleasure, my single extravagant indulgence in this shaky economy. Rubbing his forehead, I spoke softly to him and he responded by raising his foot and tapping the gate, asking for a ride. I felt inspired; why not?

In the house I tossed the mail unopened on the desk and headed to the bedroom to change. By the time I reached the doorway I was pulling my interview clothes off, discarding them and the memory of the wretched interview in the corner. I pulled on my riding jeans, a tee and a loose flannel shirt, grabbed my boots and a jacket by the back door and headed to the barn.

The barn never failed to console me; its sweet smell of grains and hay mixed with animal sweat and leather was like an intoxicant that both relaxed and invigorated me. By now Geronimo was pacing around his pen, his anticipation of the ride mirrored my own. He allowed himself to be caught, shoving his nose into the halter while I murmured words of endearment. His ears swiveled toward me, listening while keeping his gaze on the path that led to the fields.

I brushed him quickly, picked his hooves clean, smoothed the blanket over his withers and then slung the hefty western saddle up, settling it onto his back. Cinching him up, I felt my expectancy rise. Up in the saddle, I felt the knots of anxiety in my body ease as I guided him toward the recently picked field across from our property.

Our neighbor, the farmer, had given us free access to his land, and crossing the road I could see Geronimo's eyes and ears focusing on a flock of wild Canada geese gleaning in the field. These flocks were such a common sight in our area I'd barely noticed them on my way up our driveway but now I wondered how they'd react to sharing the field with us. Notoriously shy of human contact, I expected the geese to scatter and perhaps fly away, but I was surprised instead to see them watching us curiously, moving calmly aside as we passed among them, their heads reaching the bottom of my stirrups.

By now Geronimo's attention was off the geese and on the far end of the field some quarter of a mile away; his walking pace quickening. Tightening my legs and lifting the reins, I signaled him to trot and he moved instead into a loping canter. Eager to run this early fall morning, the horse snorted and blew, drawing the sweet smell of damp earth and sky deep into his chest. He wanted to run, and I knew if I let him dictate our pace he'd be hard to contain, so I corrected him, bringing him back down into a warm-up trot. Too well-mannered to disobey outright, Geronimo telegraphed his frustration by swinging his head wildly up and down; I couldn't help but grin at his antics.

At the far end of the field we rode back and forth a few times before I allowed him to ease into his lovely, rocking canter. We turned smoothly and rode back toward the road, the geese drifting like a living cloud around us once more, allowing us to pass among them. At the beginning of the field I again turned Geronimo smoothly, tested the saddle and then leaned forward.

His leap forward into a full gallop was as effortless as any automatic transmission and a rippling laugh of pure joy erupted unbidden from my lips. We flew across the ground, and as we did I took joy in Geronimo's joy, his love of movement, our symmetry, his raw power and strength. And as we enjoyed the moment, the geese around us broke into a cacophonous symphony, making it seem they were sharing our moment with us.

That night when my husband arrived home and asked me how my day had gone, I smiled and said, "I rode through a field of wild geese."

Flight 93
DeVonna R. Allison

We never know when we'll have a chance encounter or how it will affect us. Earl and I had a chance encounter with our country's recent history while returning home from the national convention a week ago. Our route took us past Shanksville, Pennsylvania, where signs directed travelers to the National Memorial of Flight 93, the infamous "fourth plane" of 911. The story of how the passengers of Flight 93 overpowered their captors, causing the flight to crash and thereby halting a suspected attack on Washington, DC, is the stuff of legends. We knew we wanted to stop.

The Flight 93 Memorial Park is located at the edge of the scenic Allegheny Mountains and despite our drive's destination, we were enjoying the breathtaking scenery. It was a beautiful sunny day with crisp 20° temperatures and I recalled, from accounts I'd read, that it had been on just such a day of clear skies and sunshine that Flight 93 was hijacked.

The park's entrance road is fittingly named Approach Road, and it winds contoured to the countryside. The park website said Sundays were the busiest days to visit the memorial, but this was a chilly, gusty Sunday in early March so the parking lot was mostly empty. We pulled on our winter coats and began our walk to the memorial.

According to a topographical map situated near the entrance, the walkway follows the exact path that Flight 93 traveled the day it went down. I wondered just how low the plane had been when it passed this spot and what must have been going on in the cockpit and the cabin.

The walkway to the memorial is also a timeline of events leading to the moment of Flight 93's crash. Engraved in the path are the times when the three other flights were hitting the World Trade Center and the Pentagon. I stepped carefully over the words, not wanting to walk on them.

The imposing outer walls of the memorial are forty-feet high of soaring concrete, angled slightly outward away from the crash site. It created a sort of wind tunnel the day we visited. The visitor center was on our left, but we continued along the flight path until the walkway ended abruptly at an overlook. There, across the valley in front of us, was the crash site, and etched on the glass wall jutting toward it were the words, "A common field one day. A field of honor forever."

We stood quietly, absorbing the scene, and I felt a little let down. It *was* common; just a windswept, mid-winter field with a granite boulder marking the point of impact in the distance. For a moment I wanted it to be different, for them, the ones who died. I wanted it to be more remarkable, but that's the point, isn't it? The *place* isn't remarkable; it's what happened there that sets it apart from the surrounding acres.

At the visitor center we were greeted by a uniformed ranger who welcomed us and directed us to the interactive displays of the center. I approached them with caution.

The first display showed the various morning news broadcasts from the day of the attacks. The reporters were telling their viewers, in stunned disbelief, that a plane had just struck one of the towers of the World Trade Center and then ... I turned my back, unable to watch as horror overtook the reporter's voices and the second plane hit. I tried not to imagine the screams, the cries, the loss ... I moved on quickly.

One display showed fragments of the plane recovered from the Flight 93 crash site. I was shocked at how small the pieces were; most were no bigger than a quarter. I began to realize the utter destruction that must have occurred at impact. One first responder was quoted as saying, "We're trained to save people ... but there was no one to save that day." That's when I realized there were no bodies to recover. There was no wreckage. There was nothing to see after the plane slammed into the meadow going over 500 miles per hour. There was only a smoldering crater at the point of impact and several fields of finely fragmented debris. The two largest pieces of the plane, found some 2,000 yards from where it went down, were said to be the "size of a dining-room table."

I spent most of my time in the visitor center, viewing the wall of photographs of those who were killed on Flight 93. That was why we'd come, after all. To pay homage to the forty people we lost that day. I viewed their smiling faces and I was pained for their families and for the lives cut short.

I felt relief when we left the visitor center, a feeling I realized I'd also experienced exiting Yad Vashem, Israel's famous Holocaust museum in Jerusalem. There's only so much suffering and loss one can absorb.

Earl and I walked back to our car in silence.

It wasn't a stop we planned, nor one we enjoyed, but we were both glad we took the time to visit the Flight 93 Memorial. It felt like we had done our duty that day by stopping and remembering.

Grit and Grace

Locked Out
DeVonna R. Allison

As soon as I closed the front door behind me, I knew I'd locked myself out. I could picture my house and car keys dangling from their hook beside the door and was instantly annoyed. After all, I had appointments to keep! Muttering to myself, I stomped around the outside of the house, checking the back door and windows, hoping to find a way inside and instead finding everything locked up tight. Rattling the back door hopefully, one last time, I heard our family dog growl menacingly at me from inside. Nice. As much as I loved our rural home in southern Michigan, it did have its downsides; we had no public transportation and our nearest neighbor was an uncomfortable hike away. Playing my last card, I crossed my fingers and went to look for the spare key that hung on a nail just inside the door of our barn; in theory, at least. The key was placed there for our notoriously absent-minded teenagers who often left home without their house key. The nail was empty, however, our teenagers also being notorious for not replacing the spare once they'd used it. It was official then, I was really locked out.

    I thumped down in the yard swing and made phone calls to the people I was supposed to be meeting and for some reason it didn't help my mood one bit that everyone I spoke to was kind and understanding when I explained I'd be unable to make our appointments. Having made the few necessary phone calls, there was nothing more I could do, so I settled back in the swing to wait for my daughter to get home from sports practice and let me back in the house. At first, my mind raced as I fretted over all the things I could and should be doing rather than wasting my time sitting in the yard. I thought of the report I needed to get ready for an upcoming meeting and the pile of laundry waiting beside the washing machine. I glanced over at my small vegetable garden, where the weeds stood like conquest flags between the peppers and tomatoes. Because I had dressed in hose and heels for my morning appointments, even yard work wasn't an option at this point. I was mid-way through a pretty good sulk when the quiet of the woods that surrounded our property blanketed me, muffling my thoughts. Chattering birds flitted through the treetops while the cicada buzz of early summer ebbed and flowed in the air around me. Our small flock of laying hens purred and chuckled softly to each other as they scratched in the dust nearby and a leafy breeze stirred. Resigned, I settled more comfortably into the padded swing, resting my head on its high back. Our cat appeared, seemed surprised to find me sitting in the morning sun and jumped lightly onto my lap, purring loudly as she settled in, rocking the swing ever so subtly. I continued the rocking motion as I waited, steeped in the modern rarity of doing absolutely nothing. Maybe it was the sight and sounds of the contented hens or the steady creaking of the swing that soothed me, but as I relaxed I became aware of a small plane humming high overhead. I watched the plane pass and my mind was drawn by the sight and sound of it, back to my great-grandmother's beach house on the shore in southern California. When I was very young, our family would visit Nana on Balboa Island in the 1960s. Those were glorious summer days; the extended family would gather and while the grownups spent their days lying on the beach or seated around the kitchen table smoking and playing cards or Yahtzee, we children would entertain ourselves with the imaginative play of our childhood.

Without television programs, videos or electronic toys, we children were perfectly happy to entertain ourselves in the blazing heat of the courtyard at Nana's house with nothing more than a ball or a jump rope. Daily a small plane would drone mechanically over the heads of the holiday crowds, trailing advertising banners. Our days were spent playing in the sun, our evenings at the carnival midway and our nights on the comfortably lumpy sofa bed on Nana's screened porch where my sunburned skin was soothed by cool cotton sheets while the calliope sounds of the distant midway floated in the air. We watched the first moon landing in 1969 at the beach house. The grownups all crowded around Nana's television, a large wooden cabinet set with a tiny black and white screen. I remembered the set smelled like hot dust after it was switched on and how we had to wait for the tubes to warm up before a fuzzy grey picture gradually formed at its center. I remembered my five-year-old self trying to imagine a man actually walking on the moon way up high over our heads. *Why* was he there, I wondered. Sitting on the swing, I was surprised at all the memories that came flooding back: I remembered playing hopscotch and tag in the scorching concrete courtyard of Nana's house; the smell of hot summer roses that grew beside the porch; and I remembered drinking icy sweet Kool-Aid out of plastic cups. One summer we discovered a new treat called "instant pudding," which we made by shaking the powdered mix with milk in sealed containers until our arms ached. I remembered the horrifying thrill of riding the Ferris wheel at night, suspended between earth and sky while cool salty air swirled about me off the black waters of the ocean. I remembered strolling the midway behind my glamorous teenaged girl cousins, one of whom had a boyfriend who met her there; I was so envious. I remembered the sound of waves, shushing against the shoreline, while we walked the few blocks home from the carnival back to Nana's house and how I drifted to sleep while the grownups talked and smoked in the next room.

It all came back so vividly and pleasingly as I sat rocking in the yard swing that when my daughter finally arrived home two hours later and teased me about locking myself out of the house, I honestly didn't mind anymore. I had briefly revisited a time of sweetness and innocence and was thinking everyone should lock themselves out of their modern lives once in a while.

Sans Air
DeVonna R. Allison

This year the central air conditioning went out in our home. For the first time in thirty years, we've sweated and dripped our way through a midwestern summer without so much as a window unit to break the heat. Here in Michigan we live nestled in the bosom of the Great Lakes and they lend their wet breath to the air and dampen every breeze.

I've taken more naps this summer, I've noticed. Afternoons find me watching the sheer drapes beside my bed sway in the breeze as if the house itself were panting in the heat. Of course, I blame the heat and crawling humidity for my lack of energy; I had experienced something like it when I spent some time in the tropics of Mexico.

There my first experience with heat-related malaise had coincided with travel on a rickety bus. The bus, nicknamed, *la vitrina*, or "the kitchen cupboard," by the locals because of its square shape and many large, untinted windows, really did resemble a kitchen cupboard. One day, my friend Norma and I traveled from the city of Tamazunchale over a treacherous switchback road to her home in Tanquian in *la vitrina*. The trip was rather long because *la vitrina* stopped frequently along the way to take on and let off passengers. Plus, the road we were traveling was in poor repair in some spots, forcing our driver to forge ahead at a rocking crawl. The bus's many windows were left wide open, allowing the intense, sticky heat to circulate, but by the time we arrived at Norma's village I was wilting quickly. I was hot, sweaty, dusty, windblown and distinctly woozy; I didn't realize it, but I was in the grips of my first tropical malaise.

At Norma's house I was relieved when she steered me toward her bedroom where she switched on a window air conditioner. I sank onto her bed as a feeble but nonetheless refreshing stream of air flowed around me. I noticed curious neighbors peering in at me through the windows. They seemed to take amusement in the sight of the *extranjera*, or foreigner, lounging in that cold air. I motioned for them to come in and join me, but they laughed and shook their heads firmly. Norma explained later that the locals believe that cold air causes sickness. It's why they fled for cover from the cooling rains when they arrived and heavily wrapped their babies even at the height of summer's heat.

Though the malaise I felt at home this summer could not compare with what I experienced in Mexico, memories of my time in that region of the world come back to me as I lie beneath the swirling ceiling fan in my bedroom in Michigan. Perhaps I should instate the afternoon siesta as part of my normal summer routine, I muse drowsily.

Something else I noticed this summer sans air was my husband softened his hard and fast rule against leaving the windows open at night. I can listen to the sounds of the summer darkness. I've become aware of the ever-so-faint traffic sounds from the highway a mile to our south, and the sounds of crickets and frogs chirping in frenzied harmony. Every once in a while a jet rumbles high overhead and I am for a moment transported in my imagination with its passengers through the night.

The air conditioning crisis has afforded us some wonderful advantages, things I had not given much thought to before. We change our bedsheets more frequently so we get to enjoy that lovely, fresh, clean feeling more often as we lay our heads down at night. Our days are quieter without the hum of the compressor unit behind the house as well. We appreciate our ceiling fans much more, and we purchased an old-fashioned box fan for the first time in years.

As soon as I switch the box fan on, the sound takes me back to childhood days when I sat on the floor in front of my grandparents' fan and spoke into the whirling blades, taking joy in the robotic alteration of my voice. This would happen at their home in Arizona, where they lived in a cement block house built by my grandpa and his grown sons. I remember how the thick walls of that house kept the fierce rays of the sun out and the inside of the house refreshingly cool. That box fan was all that was needed in the main room of the house to stir the air and keep us comfortable.

One day my grandmother made me come in from outside and offered me some lemonade. I enjoyed the lemonade, but pouted at being called inside. I had been playing with my grandparents' small black dog when he suddenly took refuge in the deep shade beneath a bush and refused to come out. I went to complain to Grandma when she told me gently, "Dolly, you leave that poor dog alone for a while. It's a 113-degrees outside..."

There's no heat in Michigan like a dry Arizona desert heat! No, here our air conditioners strip the humidity from the air, but I have memories of sitting in front of my family's swamp cooler out west. A swamp cooler is a huge square box of a contraption that draws the hot, dry outside air in through water-cooled filters. The result is a nice, cool, damp air that keeps noses and throats from drying out in the arid western heat. I used to sit in front of our swamp cooler in the summertime, taking refuge in more ways than one because I would write as I sat there—stories of cool, dark woods and fairy people and animals; all sorts of fantastical tales. Those were magical times that would break through the deep sadness of my real life and give my soul relief, just as the cooler gave my body relief.

Honestly, it hasn't been that terrible without the air conditioning. I've enjoyed the smell of sunbaked grasses coming in through the screen as aromatic as a freshly filled hay loft. I've enjoyed the unfiltered sounds of an approaching cloudburst and when at last the heat breaks and the rain spills down, the clean, damp smell of summer rain fills and cools the inside of the house. I've enjoyed reconnecting with summers sights, sounds and smells, as well as unexpectedly reconnecting with some happy memories of summers gone by.

Grandma's Baby
DeVonna R. Allison

The Winnebago pitched and groaned as it crawled the rural two-track lane split off from the main road. I was eleven years old that summer and visiting Minnesota with my grandparents. As a kid from Los Angeles, I found everything about rural life interesting, if not a bit strange.

The day's brilliant sunlight was softened by overhanging tree branches as we eased up to a small, fenced-in clearing. The chain-link seemed oddly out of place in this secluded spot, but "It keeps the deer out," my grandfather informed me. As we climbed down from the RV, I looked around, hoping to spy limpid brown eyes peering out of the surrounding foliage. What I discovered instead were headstones.

There was an unlocked gate that allowed us entrance to the small cemetery and my grandparents walked the neat rows, looking for and photographing the final resting places of loved ones from long gone. The reason for our visit escaped me at the time, but I've since come to understand their desire to document the lives of the departed. I busied myself picking wildflowers and while my fingers grew sticky from dandelion milk, my grandparents talked quietly behind me, their small black Kodak clicking. Waving aside a hovering honeybee, I concentrated on braiding the flowers' hairy stems until, finished, I went to find my grandmother, intent on displaying my handiwork. I found her standing, looking down at a small marker nestled in the sun-warmed grass. Before I could speak I noticed there were tears on her face.

"Mother, it's been years..." my grandfather spoke as he joined us.

"I know, but he was my baby." Grandma was defensive.

My ears perked up; I couldn't imagine my grandma a young mother. I looked at her, mystified, but it didn't seem to be the right time to ask questions. Instead, I laid my flowers on the baby's grave and took Grandma's hand.

Later, as we traveled the highway, Grandma and I sat at the table in the Winnebago while my grandfather drove, and I was finally able to ask her about this mysterious stranger. His name was Clark, she said. And he was born a strong, healthy baby. Unlike my own Daddy, who was born so small and weak that his paternal grandmother had taken one look at him and famously sniffed, "He'll never live." Clark grew and gained weight and delighted his small family until one morning Grandma discovered him dead in his bed. Clark had died in his sleep.

As my grandmother told me the story, her eyes took on a faraway look, and her sadness was palpable. Crib death, they called it, she said. No known reason for it, no way to predict or prevent it, it came silently into homes of the rich and poor alike and stole a little glimmer of light from them.

I wondered that I'd never heard this story before but got the impression my grandfather was uncomfortable with talk of his little son.

Years later, I buried a child of my own and through the fog of my grief I recalled my grandmother's tears and felt a special kinship with her. Though she'd been gone for several years herself by the time my teenaged son died, our shared grief united us, making us something more than grandmother and granddaughter, something more akin to sisters.

To this day, when I am ambushed by grief, when sadness and longing are stirred by some sweet reminder of my son, I am encouraged to know my grandmother wept, even thirty-plus years after her loss. From her example I learned that though grief may be arbitrary in manifesting itself, it is not to be feared or to be allowed to define me.

On the Train from Milan
Monica Clark

We stow our backpacks and six of us sit comfortably in a padded booth, three on each side, facing each other across a wide wooden table as the train from Milan lumbers down the tracks, slowly leaving the great steel and stone station with its lofty, cathedral-like ceilings.

Outside of the city, the train picks up speed and the iron rails hum their age-old song. Hale and hardy, brusque in its efficiency, the iron horse gallops through the countryside, racing past fields and valleys, tiny villages and sprawling cities. Like voyeurs, we peer into the backyards and back alleys and get a glimpse into the hidden places seldom seen by anyone but curious passengers.

The sun heats up the railcar and the day feels sleepy and lazy. We amuse ourselves, flipping cards in a ferocious game of "Golf," until hunger sends us scurrying to buy snacks from the vendor in the next car. We take our plunder back to the table and share a feast of pungent Greek olives, mozzarella cheese, paper-thin prosciutto and crusty Italian bread drizzled with virgin olive oil, a traveling picnic, a comfort for the soul and the stomach.

The train hurries across the land passing elegant, ruler-straight rows of lavender. Yellow-fringed sunflowers, their faces turned upward to the sky, trace the path of the sun. Suddenly, we are surrounded on both sides by a sea of rapeseed. Grown for oil, and a startling shade of yellow so brilliant it seems to burn into our eyes. The fields glow with a gold so pure and bright, it is as if each tiny flower somehow found a way to capture and distill sunshine. Outside every window is a feast of color.

Orchards, vineyards and olive groves glide by. Rows of cypress trees line village lanes like spears planted at the hilt. Pony carts, Vespas, tour buses and Italian sports cars sometimes race the train briefly on parallel roads.

The sky is blue and cloudless and the air shimmers with heat. The railcar sways like a gentle hammock and soon my eyelids droop. I awake a short time later, leaning against the window, sorry to have missed even a tiny bit of the spectacular view.

As the train rolls on, I know I am lucky, fortunate to be following in the footsteps of debutantes and steel lords' sons, the children of oil barons, the Rockefellers, Vanderbilts and Astors, all children of the Gilded Age, who a century ago sailed off to Europe on the Grand Tour. Now, our group: teachers, office workers, homemakers and students, everyday Americans, ride the train from Milan, headed for Rome.

There, we will explore the modern city and the ancient forum. We will stand where Caesar stood, betrayed and murdered nearly 2000 years ago. We will make a pilgrimage to the Vatican and actually see the Pope. We will explore the remnants of Circus Maximus in the moonlight, walk under the open dome of the Pantheon, and tour the Coliseum where a clowder of feral cats still roams like tiny shadows of the mighty lions that once fought fierce battles in the great arena. And finally, we will throw coins in the Trevi Fountain so that we may always return to Rome. As the train from Milan continues its journey, I am content just to be aboard.

Grit and Grace

Rabbits, Rats and Pineapples
Monica Clark

The first year we lived in our house winter buried us under three feet of snow. As temperatures dropped, harsh winds scoured the frozen lake and whipped the snow into great sculpted drifts. A raging herd of wild rabbits invaded our backyard. Okay, maybe they were not raging, and maybe they were always there, but after it snowed they were much easier to see.

Rabbits bounced over snowdrifts and played tag on the deck, but they were hungry rabbits and soon began eating the bark off our ornamental trees. So, we bought a bag of rabbit pellets and started a feeding station there on the deck. Warning: Do not try this at home!

Our son, Chris, was around eight years old, and in the evenings just before bedtime we would snuggle up under a blanket on the floor near the patio doors watching the wild antics of the rabbits as they scampered and played in the moonlight.

When they grew tired, the bunnies would hop up on the deck for a snack, where they feasted on free food just feet from our faces. It was amazing until the night Chris said, "Look, Mommy, a *baby* rabbit!"

Sure enough, a small, furry creature darted up between two rabbits, grabbed a pellet and quickly disappeared.

"Awww..." I thought at first until I realized, "Wait a minute. There should not be baby rabbits this time of year."

So I grabbed the Maglite. The back porch lit up like a prison yard during a jailbreak and there, transfixed in the flashlight's powerful beam, stood a very plump and well-fed rat. He had hit the mother lode, the greatest winter food bank ever.

Well, that was the end of feeding the rabbits—until last winter. It started with a couple of soft apples. Not wanting to scale the mountainous drifts to get to the compost heap, I stepped out on the deck, gave the wind-up and the pitch and, yes, I throw like a girl, missed the compost heap completely. The apples landed, appropriately enough, under the crabapple tree. That night, my husband, Brad, called me to the window.

A rabbit, a soft lump in the moonlight, sat holding one of the apples in his front paws, nibbling it like a little kid gnawing on an ear of corn.

"Awww."

Soon, other food scraps were sailing in the general direction of the compost heap. I can tell you for certain that rabbits are not interested in turnip ends, potato peels, wilted lettuce, soft tomatoes, orange peels or, surprisingly enough, carrots. Bugs Bunny was wrong. Nor do they care for pineapples.

How do I know this? Well, my husband cannot resist a fresh pineapple. The man is addicted. If there's a pineapple in the grocery store, it goes into the cart. Who can blame him? Few things in life are as wondrous, as sweet, succulent and juicy as a winter pineapple. Renaissance Europeans and Colonial Americans loved them. Pineapples symbolize warmth, wealth and hospitality. Their likeness can be found decorating the facades of buildings and carved into early American furniture. People know a good thing when they see it.

Word of advice, however—never, ever, ever buy a pineapple on sale. They always go to the dark side. They look fresh and inviting, but if you do not eat them that first day, the flesh turns dark and gruesome.

Well, Brad picked up the latest bad apple, aimed for the compost heap and gave it a great overhand toss but, alas, the fruit landed with a resounding, "plop!" right on top of a three-foot snowdrift in the middle of the yard.

The rabbits ignored it. For two weeks the pineapple stood straight and tall, its spiky green leaves aimed at the cloudy winter sky. A tropical fruit completely out of place in an Indiana snow bank.

Then one morning we woke up and it was gone. The snow had receded quite a bit, but there was no sign of the pineapple, no track, not a single clue to the frozen fruit's fate.

We talked about it, ruling out squirrels, possums, skunks and alien abduction. Our best guess? A raccoon. Can you imagine how it went at his house?

"So, Ralph, what did you find for us to eat for dinner?"

"I don't know, Mable, some kind of giant pinecone."

Weren't *they* in for a surprise.

There was one other possibility, I guess. The afternoon after the disappearance, my mom called. She had gotten up in the middle of the night and happened to glance out the window. There, racing across the frozen lake, trotting toward her, was some sort of doglike creature. The mystery critter ran in a straight line, right up into her yard and disappeared around the corner of her house and into the nearby woods.

"I'm not sure what it was," she said. "But it had a big, bushy tail. Might have been a fox."

I had to ask, "Was he carrying a pineapple?"

Groundhog Days
Monica Clark

I have always loved living here at the lake. The sunrises. The misty mornings. The wildlife. We have been entertained by a variety of wild creatures including raccoons, rabbits, muskrats, minks, ducks, geese, moles, voles, mice, bats, and a particularly loud and annoying ground squirrel. But this year we have a new animal on the premises.

It started on a sunny Saturday afternoon. I was home alone, relaxing on the couch with a good book, when a sudden rustling sound started outside the open patio doors. I ignored it at first, (I told you it was a good book), but the curious sound grew louder and louder, finally driving me off the couch and sending me creeping to the back door. The plastic sheeting moisture barrier under the deck that steers rainwater away from the house crackled and rattled. Something was definitely under there. Something big. Something noisy. And that Something was frantically clawing away at the plastic.

I stepped outside, quiet as a mouse. Although, I have to say, most of the mice I have encountered were not particularly quiet at all. Whatever the rather large-sounding Something was, it raced across the wooden planks just inches beneath my bare feet. I did what one does in these situations— jumped back into the house, shut and locked the door and waited for my husband to come home.

Later, Brad used the flashlight to show me where a groundhog had dug his den just under the back door. I was very relieved. No escaped lions. No bears. No wolverines. Only a groundhog. Just a silly groundhog. Easy enough to get rid of. *Oh, I was so naïve...*

We started making plans to uninvite our unwanted guest. Poison? Out of the question. Poisoning seems an awful way to die. Fireworks? Definitely not. But what?

First, we tried a homemade live trap. No luck. Didn't even catch the cat. Then we tried loud music and bright lights. I'm not sure what the neighbors thought, but the groundhog seemed to enjoy it. Maybe he was a teenager. So, we stepped up our game.

For the next few days, we aimed the garden hose down through the gaps in the deck and filled and refilled his den with water. Now, I don't know how the house foundation is holding up, but the groundhog is doing well. He is living in the lap of luxury with his own in-ground swimming pool. Just the other day we caught him stretched out on the deck sunning himself. I swear I smelled suntan lotion. It is bad enough he moved in, but now he thinks he owns the place. His personal Club Med.

Last night, however, he went too far. Last night he crossed the line. In the dark of night, under a starless sky, the furry vermin raided the garden and ate all, and I do mean all, of the ripe tomatoes. This means war!

Update: We never did see or hear the groundhog after that fateful night. He left without warning. Maybe all those tomatoes disagreed with him. Maybe an attractive lady groundhog lured him away. My personal belief is that he set off in search of an errant pineapple.

Shards
Monica Clark

The box of photos fell from the closet shelf, split at the corner and spilled colorful snapshots onto the beige bedroom carpet.

Memories erupted, sudden and violent, blocking out time and commitment, bright and bursting, crystalline shards glowing like razor-edged prisms in strong sunlight, and once again his presence lit the world.

The remembering rippled and ripped her heart. Fragments of time, the clear image of the two of them sprawled in a quiet meadow under a starburst Willa-Cather-Nebraska sky. Crickets chirruped, and the air was split by the sudden aching cry of a whip-poor-will. Night wore a perfume of sage and fresh-mown hay as wide, moon-faced cows watched the two of them sprawled on a plaid, woolen blanket. The night burned brilliant, burnished with the fiery splendor of a billion fierce stars. Two small souls lost in the magnificence.

A dream, a shadow of life. An autumn morning at the lake. The cool damp air pregnant and heady with the rich smell-taste of purple, overripe grapes. The great oaks groaned and swayed, overtaken by a massive cloud of starlings. Their harsh, raucous voices shook loose the leaves, and feathers floated and flipped, twisted and bent, like acrobats in the slanted amber light.

She picked a mottled feather from his hair and slid it in between the pages of the book he was reading. Later, she swam alone while Steven graded papers on a wobbly table in their rented cottage.

The ebb and flow of time. A torrent unleashed. That summer where they lazed, utterly contented by the sea with friends. Each of them told a story of a near-death experience. He dove once into a turquoise-blue, alpine lake, glacier-fed, and nearly cold enough to stop his heart. "It was close," he said, laughing, and she shivered as storm clouds gathered and lightning cleaved the sullen sky. The other stories are forgotten, but his she remembers. His, and the sharp, coppery smell of lightning, and the quick, changeable nature of the sea. Tranquil water turned dark and ugly. Powerful, steel-gray waves threw themselves onto shore as the storm drew near. Ragged surf pounded and beat, and the waves roiled and frothed.

And he lay still on the cold, dead sand, wrapped in a startling white sheet.

A black obsidian shard, sharp-edged and jagged. Their friends, his parents, huddled and stunned, afraid to move, afraid to speak, lest they shatter themselves on the pain that shimmered so achingly clear in the odd June heat. A solitary crow flew effortlessly across the cloudless summer sky, eyeing the fresh-turned earth—that obscene gash—where they laid him down in the churchyard under the harsh Iowa sun. A hot wind rushed across the hillside, drying her scalding tears, and the crow circled back as the first bitter fistful of dirt fell.

A vibrant tapestry turned to charcoal and ash, reduced to stained-glass memories, sweet and fleeting as summer's last lilacs. Crystal moments of sun-dappled Sundays and the smell of fresh-cut grass. Misty nights aglow with silver moonlight that turned the sycamores pale and ghostly. The joy and the wonder that was his laughter.

Sunrise. Nightfall. Starlight. A thousand slivered shards, painful and precious, burden and blessing. She gathers them all, plunges them deep into her breast and holds them there, holds them tight, until black crows fly careless circles over her.

She picks up the photographs one by one and places them carefully into the broken box.

For Steven Hershberger
March 17, 1964 – June 12, 2008.

The Holiness of Diversity
Ingrid Lochamire

There are many different varieties of trees on our 120-acre homestead, along with crops and brush, a bit of pasture and a spring-fed creek that flows year-round from the pond that never freezes over. And don't get me talking about the diversity of wildlife that thrives in our woods and around the pond. From coyotes in the far hilly field to deer in the woods to the family of ducks that shows up every spring—there's a lot going on in our corner of the world.

I keep close tabs on my surroundings, especially in spring and fall. This autumn, the sugar maple tree that stands at the side of our driveway failed to display its gorgeous golden glow. I've watched this tree celebrate the changing seasons every year for over twenty-five years. It had something to do with the weather, according to my husband, a lumberman who used to harvest hardwoods for a local mill. I don't need the science, just the assurance that next fall our beautiful maple tree will again stand tall in all its glory.

If I tended toward cynicism, I might say I wish my local faith community was as diverse as our little patch of real estate.

The church my husband and I attend has thrived for over ninety years. As the "big church" in our community, it is populated by many active and proactive attendees (we do not claim memberships). From county sheriff's deputies and teachers, nurses and doctors to business owners and farmers, accountants and lawyers, there's a lot of good work being done by these souls in our corner of the world.

There are a few Hispanics in our midst and a handful of black kids adopted by white families, but line us up next to one another and you'll see we're mostly cut from the same cloth: white, middle class, conservative. Aside from those few variations in skin color and ethnic heritage, "diverse" is probably not a word you would use to describe this congregation.

Think again.

Contrary to current vernacular, the word diversity doesn't refer only to ethnicity, sexual preference, politics or even faith traditions.

> ...*diversity – the condition of having or being composed of differing elements; variety, especially the inclusion of different types of people (such as people of different races or cultures) in a group or organization; an instance of being composed of differing elements or qualities. (Merriam Webster Dictionary)*

Looking around my church on a Sunday morning, I spot the former drug addict sitting in the front pew, tattoos peeking out from the sleeves of a biker T-shirt. This man proudly participates in a Wednesday night group to celebrate recovery.

And there's the fellow who denounced his alcoholism and accepted a role in our worship service, giving a warm hug to the seasoned lay leader who came alongside him the week he fell off the wagon, helping him forgive himself and get back on track.

There are the broken families, the pregnant single mom, the survivors of abuse, the lesbian couple and the adults with special needs who call our fellowship "family."

Other faith backgrounds are represented, too, in the young woman with roots in Catholicism, the couple who recently left the Mennonite church and a pew full of former Amish who cast off a lifestyle and mode of dress when they learned they could claim freedom in Christianity. I'm sure there are more I've yet to discover.

They're all sitting right there next to more traditional families and elderly couples who grew up in this church. All of us are learning to slide over to make room for these new believers and newcomers who lend variety, color and, yes, *diversity* to our faith family.

What I don't see when I look around my church is my Hispanic friend, the woman whose children homeschooled and attended youth conventions with my kids, the friend who knelt with me at the altar of our church on more than one occasion. Lately, she's been absent on Sunday mornings, and I miss her and her family. I miss catching her eye as she slipped into the third pew from the front, usually late and trailed by an assortment of children and grandchildren. I loved watching my friend worship. Her exuberant, off-beat clapping and spontaneous "Amen!" have been part of the fabric of our Sunday worship service for as long as I can remember.

"What happened?" I asked when we finally met up for lunch. "Where did you go?"

Over the next hour, my friend laid out her disappointment, confusion, frustration, loss. Discomfort and heartache over words, actions and attitudes of some in our church family have made her uncomfortable and have undermined the peace and harmony that are important to her in a body of believers. For her, a perceived lack of reverence and even respect for her Holy Father made our church an uncomfortable place to be.

In a way, I understood.

I grew up in The Holy Catholic Church. That's what we called it in the '60s and '70s. Today, I understand "catholic" to mean "universal" but my catechism called it "the one true church." For me, the word "church" conjures up a jumble of smells and images: polished wooden pews, smoky incense, stained-glass windows, golden altar vessels, men in priestly vestments, statues of Jesus and Mary. Add the predictable hush of prayers sung in Latin, the ringing of bells and reverential silence—all this was church. It's still the safe, insulated, isolated worship posture and style that resonate most deeply with me. If there were diverse thoughts, views, backgrounds, expectations among the congregants in the little Catholic chapel of my upbringing, I was blissfully unaware.

"Tradition!" That is the foundation my faith was built upon. I've now left behind the traditions of my childhood, but not the expectation that church should be holy, reverent, familiar and comfortable.

So I listened to my friend while she talked about her discomfort, not in agreement but in empathy. I offered no answers, no counsel that might override her choice to step away from our church. Her decision rests between her and God, and I know He will lead her. But, as I processed her frustration and disappointment, I couldn't help but wonder what brand of "diversity" is acceptable in a faith community? Which definition feels comfortable and safe within church walls?

> *"variety, especially the inclusion of different types of people (such as people of different races or cultures) in a group or organization"* or *"an instance of being composed of differing elements or qualities."*

My friend is considered an ethnic minority in our community. Her family contributes to the diversity of this small Midwestern town. But ultimately, the growing "diversity" of worship and Christian practices and the impact it has had on the atmosphere in church became a problem for her.

She's not alone. Don't all of us want to be able to manage and categorize the variances in our surroundings, in season and on schedule?

Like my expectations for our beloved sugar maple tree.

You can give me variety, Lord, but make it predictable and dependable. Don't let it clash against that which makes me feel safe and secure.

Is the flavor of diversity—*differing elements or qualities*—palatable where we do life? And just as importantly, where we worship God? Because that IS why all of us gather in our churches on Sunday mornings—to worship God, the creator of diversity in all its meanings. We are different but the same, each of us sitting here, craving the only bread that will sate our hunger.

The prophet Jeremiah wrote a letter to the Israelites living in exile in Babylon alongside a people that made them uncomfortable while they awaited deliverance. In the words of the biblical paraphrase *The Message*, Jeremiah said this:

> *"The aim of the person of faith is not to be as comfortable as possible but to live as deeply and thoroughly as possible – to live with the reality of life, discover truth, create beauty, act out love.....The only place you will ever have to live by faith is in the circumstances you are provided this very day: this house you live in, this family you find yourself in, this job you have been given, the weather conditions that prevail at this moment."*

To live deeply and thoroughly by faith in "holy diversity" is both challenging and life-giving.

Eugene Peterson, author of *The Message*, explores the life of Jeremiah in his excellent book *Run with the Horses*. He says this:

> "Exile (being with people we don't want to be with) forces a decision: Will I focus my attention on what is wrong with the world and feel sorry for myself? Or will I focus my energies on how I can live at my best in this place I find myself? It is always easier to complain about problems than to engage in careers of virtue."

We throw open the doors of our churches and say, "all are welcome." The virtuous concept of diversity, when it enters in carrying with it the weight of all its meanings, is a potent motivator to find a way to live in harmony those who don't do life (or church) in a manner or tradition we value. We're not called to compromise, but rather to adjust our expectations, even to set aside long-held preferences. The shift could mean the difference between celebrating the holiness of our differences and allowing them to divide us. Even in church.

(This essay first appeared in *The Redbud Post*)

The Way It Is with Children
Ingrid Lochamire

On a fresh-washed April day twenty-five years ago, I sat alone in my car in a rural driveway. A "For Sale" sign was planted in the front lawn. Towering before me was a brick house with white pillars rising from a broad porch. Shielded by a budding maple tree, windows rolled down to catch a whiff of spring on the breeze, I listened. Over a cacophony of bird song, I heard it—water bubbling and tumbling, gurgling with laughter in a steady cadence rising from somewhere on the hillside.

Beyond the maple tree, I spotted a rusty round cistern tucked among young green cattails. Water pooled inside the cistern and flowed down the grassy bank. Stepping from my car, I stood where I could trace the sparkling water's journey from the base of the cistern, over rocks and into a narrow creek that flowed forcefully yet gracefully, cutting a swath in the green grass beyond the driveway.

Water, spilling into the cistern and tumbling over rocks, hammered out a tune that was a balm to my anxious spirit. Standing in the sunshine, I knew. This could be home, and it could be good.

A thirty-something town girl, trading the life of a single mother to become the wife of a farmer and leaving the excitement of a career for the maternal joys of nurturing and nesting, had finally come home.

In the months ahead, the spring-fed creek and brick farmhouse embraced me, my new husband and our blended family. Springfield Farm, our farm, became a place where we learned together, birthed a family business and raised a passel of boys.

I didn't know it then, but our move to the country also ushered me into a personal season of rebirth and renewal, of spiritual growth pushed along by trial and sorrow, enriched by new friendships and a deeper relationship with my Savior.

In the years that followed our settling into the big brick house on the hillside, the creek offered a playground for our boys. Shaded by elm, walnut and maple, twig-and-bark vessels floated and tumbled over rocks. Bare feet tingled in the cold stream and dried on sun-warmed banks. The creek created a boundary for young explorers who were warned, "Go as far as the creek. No further." As they grew, the narrow waterway became a trail for confident adventurers who traced its passage under the road and across the field to merge with a larger ditch, then a river and finally, a lake.

Our piece of land is rich with history. Springfield Township was named for the springs on this property. As one of the earliest landowners in LaGrange County, Indiana, ("la grange" is French for "the farm"), the man who first settled here was influential in the formation of our county. His property was carved out of the eastern side of a glacial valley and was among the first to be platted. He set a sturdy frame house into the hillside, along with a bank barn and out buildings. When his first house burned down, he erected a "newer" brick home to take its place, marking it with a little cement cornerstone tucked high under the porch roof, dated 1876.

Buildings and ownership have changed over the years, but for centuries this piece of earth has been fed by the springs and the powerful vein of gurgling water that slices our property in half. At least five other springs of water are scattered throughout the entire one hundred-plus acres under our names in the county registry. One has been used to water livestock, while others have brought ruin to foundations or turned grassy slopes into spongy swamps. Another has pushed away flora to lay down a shallow pond, a sanctuary for muskrats, herons, tadpoles, snakes. The springs of water instill an identity to Springfield Farm, and to my family now rooted in its history.

On my morning walks, stepping across the little wooden bridge settled onto narrow shores of the creek by one of our sons so many years ago, or walking through a recently constructed covered bridge on my way to the cabin on the bank of the pond, I think of those who played here in these waters, both my own offspring and those of generations past. Like this persistent little trickle, they've carved a path into a wider waterway, into a world outside my vision. Some took a turn back and settled, like the pond, into permanency. Still others pushed far beyond the boundaries of township or county or state, wending their way to destinations foreign to us, now home to them.

The German poet Rainer Maria Rilke once opined "May what I do flow from me like a river, no forcing and no holding back, the way it is with children."

Perhaps he stood on the banks of a little creek like mine as it flowed into a river and observed "the way it is with children" who dangle their feet in shallow currents then step ashore, into life "no forcing and no holding back."

As I stand barefoot, cold water tumbling over my toes, pressing against my ankles, I wonder:

What I do—writing, mentoring women, advocating for healthy relationships, supporting my husband as he builds a business, walking alongside our adult children—does it flow from me like a river? Or is my labor forced, performed as an obligation rather than a privilege? And do I hold back in some misdirected scheme of self-protection, throwing obstructions of my own making into the river, impeding my progress, resisting strong currents?

As women chasing after God, we know what happens when we resist the plans of our Creator, the One who has "made known to (us) the paths of life" and promised to "fill us with joy in his presence" (Acts 2:28). Opportunities are missed. Blessings delayed. Joy denied.

When we step toward God without fear, when we cease striving and become like children, living with abandon and trusting the current of His promises, it's then we find the path he's mapped out for us.

Lord, you have placed me here, on the bank of a waterway that connects me to so many others, past, present and future. You have laid out a path for my life. You have given me an existence that calls me to reach out, to trust others and to walk in faith as you direct me to territories unplanned and unknown. You have opened pathways I could not have designed for myself, some littered with heartache, others shining with blessings. Lord, may I not force my will into your providence. At the same time, may I cease holding back, protecting myself from what I can't control. Show me, as a woman who seeks to please and honor you, how to relish the gift of faith that was placed in me at the moment of salvation. May I claim it as an inheritance that pays benefits every day of my earthly life. I hold in my heart gratitude for the overflowing promise of grace and mercy that carries the righteous toward an eternal home.

Coffee Break
Ingrid Lochamire

Eleanor Roosevelt said, "Do one thing every day that scares you."

I spent a year as a barista in my favorite coffee shop. The days I donned my coffee house tee-shirt and stepped behind the counter were a pleasant kind of scary and they challenged me in ways that caused an adrenalin rush. Just learning to run a digital cash register was worth the year I worked at the coffee shop.

Though I no longer clock in at 6:30 a.m. to serve coffee, I learned plenty that I've applied to other challenges I'm taking on in this final quarter of my earthly life—things like understanding people and their motivations.

A couple of years ago, a contributor to the website Buzzfeed compiled a list of thirteen different types of people you see in coffee shops. At my coffee shop, I encountered most of them:

1. The stressed-out college student
2. The professional
3. The person with the super-complicated order that holds up the line
4. The barista who can't spell anyone's name right
5. The intern getting coffee for her boss
6. Moms escaping their kids
7. Moms who can't escape their kids
8. The hipster
9. The would-be novelist
10. Jobless young adults who have nothing better to do
11. The cute couple who makes you want to vomit

12. The person who may be homeless, or may just be unkempt
13. The actual homeless guy

Another list I found added the "true coffee-addict" who says "just give me the coffee" then darts out the door or into a dark corner.

One thing most of these types have in common is that they are just happy to be there. They're giving themselves a break and they usually feel pretty good about it. For many coffee shop customers, it's not all about the coffee. Just as sharing a meal around a common table is an act of communion, sipping a cup of coffee or tea in a cozy spot with a positive vibe and a good view holds an element of self-care that's healthy for body and soul.

Pausing for refreshment is like taking a deep breath and saying, "I'm worth this. I need it and I deserve it." Self-care is highly underrated in our crazy, get-ahead world. Stepping off the treadmill for a moment to sit across the table from a friend, read a book or even socialize in the cyber world while nursing a special cup of coffee or a frozen smoothie isn't a bad thing. In fact, people might be a lot happier if they built an occasional coffee break into their lives.

The Work of Grandma's Hands
Traci Rhoades

Idle hands make one poor, but diligent hands bring riches.
Proverbs 10:4

Lucy's hands were always hard at work. Married at nineteen, she started having babies right away, only taking a few years off in between before calling their family complete at seven children. One baby keeps a mama's hands busy enough, but seven? Her husband, Carroll, worked the fields and cared for the animals on their farm in rural Missouri, so he had his hands full as well. She told him early and often, "Your work is outside, and I'll be in here taking care of the house and the children."

Meals were simple but always on the table in time, comprised of meat and vegetables from the farm. It wasn't unusual to have steaks for dinner because they raised their own cattle, and each butchering offered up various cuts of steak. Her arsenal of meals also included meatloaf, hamburger patties and breaded pork tenderloin fried in the skillet. The meat always had a side of vegetables—they were grown in the summer months, canned in the fall and feasted on year-round—and also homemade macaroni and cheese on occasion. A platter of pickles was usually placed on the table. They didn't have much in the way of store-bought. On Sunday nights, the special dinner was corn cakes with sliced tomatoes and a side of milk—fresh milk from the dairy cows.

Carroll always set his wind-up alarm clock for 5:00 a.m. to do his chores. Lucy slept in for at least another hour before making the family a breakfast of sausage and eggs. After cleaning up from the morning meal and getting the kids off to school, Lucy often made a pie or cookies to satisfy Carroll's sweet tooth. Fresh lemonade and later Kool-aid were always on hand as well to quench his thirst for sugary refreshment. Food was readily available on the farm and Lucy's hands lovingly prepared it for her crew.

Carroll and Lucy were my maternal grandparents. Mom and her siblings all have good memories of farm life, although what they remember varies a great deal depending on their birth order. Some liked to work outside in the fields and with the animals, while others preferred to stay in and help with household chores. If you ask my aunts, they're quick to point out which ones were willing to do what. The ones who stayed inside helped Grandma Lucy, and there was always work to do.

With seven children, the Bennett family gave quite a boost to overall attendance at the small Methodist church where they worshiped on Sunday mornings. As neighbors, they were always willing to lend a helping hand, or a helping child if needed, and stayed active in their community. It's this community that supported them when their third child, Norma Jean, lost a leg in a farming accident at age five. Grandma Lucy traveled with her daughter to Shriner's Hospital in St. Louis after the incident. For a time, her hands were needed elsewhere. The community stepped in to help with things at the farm temporarily. Over the years, it was the local Shriner's organization who raised the money to outfit Norma Jean with new prosthetic legs as she grew.

This same community came together to grieve the loss of not one, but two, of Grandma Lucy's teenage children. Norma Jean and the oldest son, Sammy, died within a year of one another. Even though my mom was only eight or nine at the time, she remembers this being such a sad time, with lots of weeping. Grandma Lucy's hands set out to do a different kind of work in those tragic days. They closed the lids of two caskets. It was the hardest work her hands ever had to do; nothing in life had prepared her for that. Grandma Lucy's hands went still for a time, along with the rest of her, as she went deep inside herself to mourn.

For weeks, she prepared some meals, but left a good deal of the cooking and housework up to her older daughters. Neighbors and family came by to visit, but no one knew what to say. Granddad tried his best to visit with the people who dropped in to offer their condolences. Grandma Lucy came out of her bedroom from time to time and sat on the couch. Sitting silently among those loved ones who remained, tears flowed down her cheeks. Had she known she would sit at the casket of another son years later, or care for a husband who deteriorated before her very eyes from Alzheimer's disease, or provide a home for an aging parent in her final days, I'm not sure she would have stayed sane. In the Lord's wisdom, he doesn't reveal the ways we'll suffer all at once.

In time, Grandma Lucy set aside her grief and went back to living. In their church, there wasn't a lot of talk about "having faith" or a "personal relationship with Jesus." For Grandma Lucy, faith meant action. She had five other children to raise and putting those hands to work again felt better than getting swallowed up by grief. What choice did she have? After the accidents, she didn't talk about my Uncle Sammy or Aunt Norma Jean unless someone else brought them up. I guess reliving their too-short lives would have been too difficult.

Working hard was all Grandma Lucy knew, and she determined if her growing kids were to have the money they needed for school and other activities, and if they were to have nice, albeit hand-made clothes, she needed to earn some extra money. My grandparents weren't looking to get rich—everyone around them was poor—but she wanted to help her family do more than just get by.

Grit and Grace

As a farmer's wife, Grandma Lucy raised chickens and sold their eggs. Dozens of fresh eggs were kept in cases in the garage until local buyers stopped by to purchase them. She sold milk as well. It was put in large cream cans, placed in a water cooler down near the road, and someone picked the milk up every few days. I remember seeing these large cream cans painted as home decor at craft shows in the 1980s—functional turned fashionable.

Perhaps Grandma Lucy's most successful venture was in direct sales for the Stanley Company. In the 1960s, before house parties were a thing, she sold Stanley Home Products in the homes of her friends. Many nights, she'd leave my mom and her younger brother, Lonnie, at home with their dad to go do a house party. The utility room in the back of their farmhouse often had boxes of product that needed to be sorted into bags for the hostesses to distribute. She did very well in this endeavor, even earning enough credit to give my mom a set of fine China dishes as a wedding gift.

For a time, Grandma Lucy also sold Sarah Coventry Jewelry. I always enjoyed going through her jewelry boxes as a little girl, and on more than one occasion I wondered why she had such unique, fancy pieces. I always knew Grandma Lucy to be a simple country lady. However, she'd earned a lot of free jewelry over the years, and although she didn't have many occasions to get dressed up, Mom recalls her always wearing nice jewelry to church and to her house parties.

Grandma Lucy even raised chinchillas in her basement and sold them for profit. Dozens of their cages were stacked in a side room at the bottom of the basement stairs. They required daily cleaning, food and water. No one seems to remember who bought these creatures from Grandma Lucy. Their fur was considered a luxury, not an item that would be in high demand in the rural community they called home. Grandma Lucy had no interest in pets of any kind—her hands stayed plenty busy caring for little people—but for a time, she tended to those rodents.

When I was growing up, Grandma Lucy still did some sewing, which eventually segued into quilting. Each member of our family has a quilt made by her hands, and my daughter received the final piece she ever completed. It's one oversized panel with a bunny on a white background and blue floral material on the back. She also crocheted, and we all have one or two doilies made by Grandma Lucy. She and my mom took jobs wallpapering and painting houses and she did this well into her 60s. Those hands could do almost anything, it seemed.

In addition to finding ways to earn extra money, Grandma Lucy also spent much of her time finding ways to save it. In the musty-smelling room of the basement where she'd once housed the chinchillas, she eventually set up a table and shelves where she could sort coupons and grocery labels for cash rebates and other products. She also kept grocery items in this room when she found a deal, or any household product she would purchase in bulk before a coupon expired. Every Christmas, she'd prepare care packages for her adult children using the goods she'd collected that year. I also remember one year, when Atari first came out, all our families saved box tops off a certain brand of cereal, and she mailed in enough to get each family a new gaming system.

Grandma Lucy hosted all our family gatherings for years, and, as always, her hands stayed busy in the kitchen. I can see her even now in my mind, standing behind the oval wooden dining room table. There's newspaper spread out on the table, and flour covering the news articles. With her rolling pin, a kitchen knife, and those hands, she's making homemade noodles, like no one has ever made before her or since.

With all her heart and her two hands, Grandma Lucy loved her family. They didn't have a lot monetarily, but life was so very rich. She always had time for her grandkids—there were fifteen of us in all and each has stories about sleepovers at Grandma's house. Although she must have grown weary with age, she always kept a pleasant demeanor. I don't recall her ever being grumpy or critical. Looking back on her life in its various stages, and knowing the depth of my own love for family, I realize she showed a tremendous amount of resolve. I carry some of that in me.

Grandma Lucy eventually moved into a small house in town, but it never really seemed like her "home" to me. The days on the farm remain the happiest memories I have of her. I can still see her walking into the living room after spending countless hours in the kitchen and looking out the big picture window at all her grandkids playing in the front yard. The fruits of her labor.

A few months after giving birth to my daughter, I traveled from Michigan to Missouri so my side of the family could meet the new baby. I couldn't wait to introduce my little girl to this woman who loved her family so well. One afternoon, we visited Grandma Lucy at the rest home where she spent her final days. I dressed our daughter in a denim jumper (it seemed most appropriate). I made sure she was bathed and fed, not wanting her to be fussy when she met her great-grandma. I entered the room Grandma Lucy shared with another lady, and I handed her my daughter, whose middle name is Carroll, after my granddad. She took her with those hard-working hands and settled the baby in her lap. Guess what my girl did in those arms, all safe and secure? She turned her body to lie down and she fell asleep. Even a baby could sense these hands would do anything for our family. She found great comfort in that, and she rested.

Memoir

Like a Phoenix
Ingrid Lochamire

I will never forget the first time I sat with my son while he was experiencing a panic attack. Everything in me wanted to hold him and make it stop. All I could do was pray and wait for it to pass.

Our adventurous, confident, athletic and creative son had his first collision with anxiety and panic in his early twenties. It came out of nowhere. He had moved from Indiana to Nashville, Tennessee, and was enjoying the city with all its new experiences and friendships. Though he'd had periods of mild depression in the past, anxiety and panic were something new. The first time he experienced anxiety was confusing and frightening, but it passed and he lived mostly anxiety-free for the next five years.

About two years ago, the feelings returned and this time, they settled in. By the time he began talking openly about it, anxiety had almost become a way of life and he lived in fear of the next panic attack.

In one life-changing year, he ended a long-term relationship and made a big career move, giving up a secure job for a promising opportunity with a major Nashville record label. The work was demanding. His anxiety escalated. Depersonalization—the feeling that he was observing himself from outside his body— became his new normal.

At the end of the summer, our son lost his new job because of limitations caused by his condition, and he crashed. That's when he made the most difficult decision of his life—he moved home to the farm, knowing he needed help.

"As the heavens are higher than the earth, so are my ways higher than your ways and my thoughts than your thoughts." Isaiah 55:9

I clung to that verse while casting frantically about for medical doctors, homeopaths, psychiatrists, counselors, anyone who could offer our son more than a prescription. While I trusted God had a plan in allowing this to come into our son's world and into our lives, I wanted to know why.

Had our son come home with a broken arm, even a broken heart, I would have known what to do. But a broken spirit? I had no answers.

Together, my husband and I talked about options and we committed to walk alongside him in this, just as we would if he had cancer or a serious injury. We made space in the house that had been an empty nest for the past three years and welcomed our son home.

What none of us knew is that statistically nearly one-fifth of my son's generation (millennials born between 1980 and 2000) reportedly suffer from some form of anxiety. (www.healthstatus.com)

Daily, we watched our son struggle to pull himself away from the depression that threatened to engulf him. He was both comforted by being in the home where he grew up, and disappointed that he was one of "those guys" who lived in their parents' spare bedroom. We kept reminding him that this was just a reset and that he would get on the other side of it. He'd get his life back.

There's an adage that says, "A mother is only as happy as her unhappiest child." Though I can't fully understand what he's living with, I have carried his pain like a heavy cloak around my shoulders. I would give anything if I could take it from him and bear it myself.

Many nights during his first weeks at home, I fell asleep pleading with God to release our son from this prison. My answers came in the mornings, and they weren't the ones I expected. Day after day, I could sense the Lord drawing me to acceptance, to peace, to calm, to unconditional servant love for our son. My anxious spirit was not helping our son, and it wasn't showing him what I believed in my heart—that God was with him in his illness and He was already there, waiting for him in his healing.

My nightly prayers turned from lament to praise. I began visualizing my son whole and healthy and thanking God for that outcome, claiming it in the name of Jesus. In my morning time with the Lord, I wrote notes to myself in my prayer journal:

> "Healing will not come in my timing."

> "Prayer stretches faith."

> "In the depression and anxiety, my son will find the God who loves him."

> "God is faithful. He will answer our prayers."

And God showed me things I could do to assist my son in his healing:

- Stop looking at him as if he's broken.
- Stop always asking him if he's okay.
- Make myself aware of the clues that he is struggling and respect that.
- Extend grace when his condition limits his productivity or interaction.
- Gently guide him to habits that can help him break through or at least help him endure depression.

- Talk about things that are positive.
- Ask his opinion and solicit his help around home where practical.
- Speak of my own hope and confidence in a positive outcome.
- Encourage and facilitate "active waiting."
- Listen without judgement and share my thoughts without always offering solutions.

While receiving treatment, our son started a small business setting up a woodshop in the garage where he builds skateboards, small pieces of furniture and gifts (while my snow-covered car sat in the driveway). He also began working a couple of hours every afternoon in our family business. And he's making plans to move to Detroit, a city on the rise, as soon as he's on his feet.

A young man on the rise taking up residence in a city on the rise—the symbolism is not lost on his family.

Our son is on a journey toward health and wholeness. He no longer uses alcohol to self-medicate, he has improved his diet and, while still taking anti-anxiety medication, he's receiving long-term therapy that is slowly bringing change.

But most importantly, he is clinging to God. He's opened his heart to the faith that he had shoved to the background. He's looking for God's purpose in this and planning for the day when he's fully functioning and living again on his own.

In his own words (from a song he wrote recently):

"I lost both my legs; I was fallin' down.
I faked it anyway.
I was fadin' away with no sound.
I can't wait anymore for my crown."

Every day, I claim these promises for him and for me:

> *"Yet the Lord longs to be gracious to you; he rises to show you compassion. For the Lord is a God of justice. Blessed are all who wait for him."* Isaiah 30:18

> *"'For I know the plans I have for you,' declares the Lord, 'plans to prosper you and not to harm you, plans to give you hope and a future.' "* Jeremiah 29:11

Postscript: Jamison is now living in Detroit and working at a job he loves. He still goes through periods of intense depersonalization and occasional depression. Daily, he chooses to look not at where he's been, but how far he's come.

(This essay first appeared in *The Redbud Post*.)

Black Birds
Ingrid Lochamire

They visited several times this week.

Black birds swooped in to fill the branches of our trees, their "caws" echoing across the valley. The first morning of their arrival, I answered their call and stepped onto the porch. Suddenly, I found myself transported back in time.

The black bird invasions have always been an event in our otherwise quiet autumn days. My sons, bent over the day's schoolwork, were summoned to the front porch by the cackle of the flock. Pencils rolled across the floor as the screen door swung open and the boys tumbled out, happy for the momentary reprieve from sums and stories. We stood there quietly and marveled each time at so many black creatures. Hundreds of them, according to our estimation, perched on tree branches or scattered across our lawn.

They raised a ruckus. How could we not join the party?

It always seemed the birds chose the brightest, most golden days of autumn to make their appearance. In the glow of ripened corn and shimmering maples, we shared the moment, the gift of nature's comings and goings, the ebb and flow of the seasons.

This morning, as the cawing again beckons me to the porch, I find myself standing alone, feet planted at a bittersweet crossroads. Moments earlier, the grey morning mist had parted as my youngest son's car rolled out our driveway, keeping an appointment to take an important test, one that marks the end of his high school career ... and my role as homeschooling mom. I have no doubt he's prepared, and I send up a prayer that he passes with flying colors.

He's ready, but am I?

Our nineteenth year of learning together at home has ended abruptly with my son's decision to turn that corner, close that chapter and gear up for what lies ahead. Abruptly, according to my calendar. Right on time, according to his.

It's the season, I know, but couldn't we just stay here a little longer? There are books to be read aloud together. Continents yet to be explored. Important issues to be discussed. Great works of art to be copied and examined.

The birds are gathering to take flight. Our "rest stop" has met their needs and they've summoned strength for the next leg of their journey. As I step back into the warmth of our home, I remind myself that they'll be back. They know where we live. They will remember that they can find rest here.

Those birds ... and my sons.

A Season of Miracles
Ingrid Lochamire

In a season of miracles, would God do less than deliver when asked? Even on a day when life is spinning wild with errands with that mad rush toward a day for celebration. Even when it's only a worried mother asking that the search for what is lost might have a good ending.

An afternoon romp in the melting snow for the pup seemed like a good idea. Snow is new to him and his winter coat hasn't thickened, but he is silly with the excitement over this new world. He stays near the barn at first, following the family dog to trace crazy circles across the yard while a foggy mist draws the day toward dusk. But soon the family dog is waiting at the front door and the pup is not at her side. We call. He doesn't come.

Darkness is falling, and the fog lays heavy on the doorstep. We wrap ourselves in coats, pull on the boots and grab flashlights. We fan out across the farm, into the hills behind the house, calling out for the pup. Husband takes the car to drive slowly down our country road, hoping he won't find what he is looking for in the grassy ditches. Turning into a field, he drives along the fence, shining his lights, window rolled down in the cold mist, whistling but hearing no bark in return.

My son ventures deep into the barns, shining his light into corners filled with sawdust, hoping he'll see the brown mound of fur hunkered down for a nap. We holler and whistle, leaving our own crazy circles in the sloppy snow.

For an hour the three of us search, coming back together to ask:

"Did you check there in the shed?"

"Didn't I hear barking at the neighbors?"

We keep our phones with us, calling to report with anxious voices. Nothing yet.

We join forces and drive into a far field, along a creek bank, following what can only be seen in our headlights. Tracks—not deer or possum, possibly dog tracks? Into the woods and out again, across the field and back. More crazy circles in the snow.

Another fifteen minutes pass. Another field and more tracks. My son jumps out of the car again and again to inspect new tracks. He hops out a final time, determined to follow them. Into tall grasses, under low bushes, he shines his light. Our hunt is futile, I fear, and I think to ask that we turn back. But he persists, calling as he swings his flashlight toward the creek.

So I pray, as I've been praying through this long evening.

"Please, God," I say again. "Please show us where he is."

I'm as worried for our son who won't give up the search as I am for the one who is lost. This search, I can see, it holds meaning for him. Searching for what is lost. He can't let it go.

And I whisper again, "Please, God. A miracle. A Christmas miracle."

I pray believing. God wants this. He wants a good ending.

Suddenly, I hear my son laugh, hear him say the pup's name, crouching low, calling softly to the lost one who is shivering with fear and cold. Son coaxes him from under the tree, scoops him into his arms and tucks him under his coat. He is speaking to the bundle, voice full with emotion. "I'm sorry," he says. "You're okay. I'm sorry."

And my tears flow because God has answered. I'll take this Christmas miracle.

Nashville
Ingrid Lochamire

The slap-crack of skateboards hitting cement punctuates the air. The town park vibrates with laughter, conversation, dog yelps, honking horns.

Overhead, dark clouds roll, hanging low, heavy with moisture soon to be dumped on the valley, already green and lush from days of spring rain. You can almost hear growth

On this spring day, there is no sun to warm my old bones or the moss-streaked slab beneath my backside. Resting against a budded sapling, I've claimed a perch and protection, rest and seclusion. It's a very public place for reflection, I think, for grappling with fresh maternal insights. But my seat in nature affords a shielded view of the skate park and my man/child at play.

This is not home turf. I am an interloper in a place that has been adopted for a time by my son, this one who carries with him the essence of home and a piece of me. A country boy, transplanted from Indiana farmland to the mecca for "country," he grapples, too, with understanding why he's here again, in the center of Tennessee, in a city he's come to know like the back of his hand. Nashville is charming, to be sure, and the new job is rewarding. But are charm and work reason enough to return?

Squeals from a little one riding piggyback on her mama ring out. An older, carbon copy of the baby sister scrambles to the top of a rock, calling out to Daddy, "See me?!" Daddy, hands shoved in the pockets of his khaki shorts, turns his head, nods and resumes his pacing. Mama and the daughters play. Daddy looks to the gathering mounds of gray overhead. Is he calculating when the drops will begin? Or wondering when he can safely take his leave of "family time" to retreat back to the house?

It may be the leaving, not the returning, that is the impetus for my offspring's rebound to this spot so far from home. Leaving the nest that has been a refuge, perhaps once too often, from the trials and realities of life, he's found his way back here to a city that has become his pseudo-home. This time, he goes it alone. No roommates, no big house full of other voices. Just himself and three empty, white rooms in an upstairs apartment in a trendy neighborhood. It was a lucky find—or perhaps a sign? Houses like this near the university never have rooms to let midterm, with a six-month lease, no less. He snatched it up, sight unseen, and now he's here.

Six weeks into his return and he's making moves that resemble nest-building. On our visit to a thrift store, he picked up some secondhand drinking glasses, a matted photograph of New York City, a small sofa. A positive sign, I say, though he declares he's taking it six months at a time

My son needs this, I think—a visit from the one who's known him from the womb, who can read his face and hear what he doesn't say. Providence, not planning, has brought me here at a time when he's facing the unraveling of an important relationship. His world has been tilted off its axis and he's looking for a way to right himself.

Mature parents, two late-in-life darlings in tow, stride down the path. "That is the absolute worst thing you could do!" The mother's reprimand halts her daughter's exploration. "Put that down! Now we'll have to wash your hands." Mother resists as her toddler tugs. "I explained this to you very carefully. This is a walk, not a 'carry'." The toddler runs ahead, stumbles and reaches to Father. "What is it,

Angel? Are you hurt?" She doesn't cry, but makes her plea, lifting her arms. "She's requesting a carry," he yells to Mother. Mother shakes her head "no" but Father lifts the toddler into his arms.

Droplets of rain stain the rocks of my shelter. I spot my son as he tips his skateboard with his toe, grabbing the board under his arm, a signal he's ready to leave. With the ollies, the board slides, the tumbles onto cement that leave their mark, endorphins have done their job. His young body has worked to relieve tension and he's been able to think. It shows in his face, in the squaring of his shoulders.

Rising, I square my own shoulders and move in his direction. I can't suppress the affectionate smile that spreads across my face. He looks exhausted, but relaxed. He looks better.

Rain begins falling steadily as we run to the car. My son tells me he needed this skate time. "Thanks for being patient," he says. We start talking of food. It's good to be focused on present, carnal needs, setting aside the "what ifs" and "what's ahead." We're here and now. And something tells me he doesn't need "a carry." He just needs me to see him.

In the rain, we drive home.

Redeeming Mother's Day
Ingrid Lochamire

I've spent a lifetime trying to figure out what to do with Mother's Day.

My birth mother left her young family on a warm summer afternoon. Her daughters were ages three, two and one. Three sisters, huddled together on our front lawn, watching our mother walk out the front door, across our yard and down the street. Our slender, beautiful mother with the deep brown eyes, dark curly hair and a skirt that swayed when she walked. She was carrying a suitcase.

In my reconstructed memories, she never looked back. My baby sister sat beside me in the dirt, crying, but my eyes stayed fixed on the back of my mother as she got smaller and smaller.

I was the oldest, but still so very young and so confused. Where was she going? Why couldn't we go with her?

I didn't know it would be several years before I would see my mother again, and that the day would come when I could only call her by her first name—Anita

My parents married when Anita was just out of high school. Barely eighteen and the oldest in a Catholic family of five children, Anita said she felt like an outsider in her own family—the illegitimate step-sister from an absent father. My grandmother had married a "good boy" when Anita was just a baby and quickly filled her house and her life with four more children.

Dad was six years older than Anita. He had just returned to his hometown following an enlistment in the United States Air Force when they started dating and married after a whirlwind romance. Photographs show a dashing, cocky young soldier and a spirited beauty with high cheekbones and those deep brown eyes. In a little more than three years, he and his teenaged bride had three babies, one right after the other.

In the days after Anita walked down the street and didn't look back, the faces of my two grandmothers replaced hers. I loved their attention, but they weren't my mother. I remember Dad crying and visits from people I barely knew. They came to our house with sad eyes, food and offers of hugs.

Dad hired an elderly family friend to stay with us while he worked at the post office in our small town, a job he'd taken after the service. Where Anita went and what she did after she left our brown-shingled house on Cherry Street remained a mystery for years. At some point, I was told she had left to search for her birth father, the man who had abandoned my pregnant grandmother before Anita was born. It was hinted that my mother had suffered a nervous breakdown and spent time in a hospital. Wherever she went, Anita didn't return for the divorce and custody hearings. My sisters and I officially had just one parent: Dad.

My father remarried when I was six years old, taking as his wife Anita's cousin by marriage, a niece of Anita's stepdad. I liked her and was excited about getting a new mother, but it was years before I could sort out the tangled relationships that came with the marriage. A new grandma who was also a great-aunt isn't an easy thing to explain to a six-year-old.

Anita slipped back into my world not long after Dad remarried. The first time I remember seeing her again, I was standing at a storm door window with my younger sisters, face-to-face with Anita. She was bent low so she could peer through the glass, trying to tell us something. We were at an aunt's home and the aunt pulled us away and shut the wooden door. Anita left, but she didn't give up trying to see her daughters. Soon, my sisters and I were being sent to visit her on weekends. In the beginning, we met at my grandmother's house on Main Street. Eventually, she took us to a nearby city where she rented a house.

Anita's life was very different from the one I lived. There was talk of a boyfriend who was in jail. She visited him and wanted us to meet him some day. I hoped we wouldn't, and we never did. Other men came in and out of Anita's life. Friends, she said, but I didn't like how they made me feel.

There were other things that frightened and confused me about Anita. Once, on a weekend visit to her house in the city, Anita drove with us in the back seat of her car through the dark of night to an alley behind a brightly lit building. She parked the car and locked us inside.

"Be good. I'll be right back," she said. Her face looked sad and I wanted to see her smile, so I nodded and pulled my little sisters close. I was afraid she wouldn't come back.

Anita disappeared through a door at the back of the building. In a little girl's mind, minutes can turn into hours and it seemed forever before she reappeared. Her sadness was gone; she was smiling and seemed happy to see us. When I was with Anita, all that mattered was that we made her happy.

My family with Dad and my stepmother was growing. I was nine when a tow-headed baby girl joined us, and two years later our family became complete with the birth of my little brother. We were the five Wilson kids, all tucked into the little stone house at the edge of town where we had moved when Dad remarried. There was barely a seam where our family had been knit together.

I found it easy to deny we were a "blended" family at all. My stepmother was "Mom" and I called my birth mother by her first name. Anita's presence in my life defied the happy family image I cherished. As my contentment at home grew, so did my resentment over being forced to visit her on weekends.

In adolescence, my heart slammed the door on Anita's claims as my mother. I refused to visit her.

A child of the '50s, I grew up on images of happy families with one mother and one father gathered around the kitchen table. Ozzie and Harriet and *Leave It to Beaver* were the models for what a good family should look like. My "abandonment" (as I chose to call it) by my birth mother came at a time when society deemed it the mother's job to raise her children. Men leaving their families, while scandalous, was not unheard of. Women didn't give up custody of their babies. Once I realized what had happened in my family, I acquired an attitude of righteous indignation over Anita's leaving.

By the time I entered my teens, Anita had remarried. She and her husband adopted two children and moved from the city to a house on the other side of our hometown. To make matters worse, they bought a bar in town.

Now Anita was a bartender. I was humiliated.

I couldn't understand why my two sisters still spent weekends with Anita and her new family, or why my parents would let them. I tolerated occasional visits with her, but I never let Anita think I wanted to be there. Instead, my pain and confusion became a hard shell that prevented me from showing her any emotion other than indifference.

As only an awkward, self-absorbed thirteen-year-old could, I tried my hardest to make Anita feel her attention was unwanted. I remember a Christmas gift of fishnet stockings, along with a pleated wool skirt and sweater. The outfit was perfect. I tried it on but refused to wear it to Christmas dinner with my grandmother. Anita had tried, but the affection of her oldest daughter could not be bought with gifts—even something as cool as fishnet stockings.

I graduated from high school and moved out into the bigger world of college, and my views on life and relationships broadened. I could look objectively at my awkward family dynamics, and I began to wonder about this woman who was my mother by birth. With the enlightenment that came as a young woman living in the '70s, I considered the realities Anita had faced as a mother of three babies before she turned twenty. I thought about what it must have been like to never have known her real father and to want desperately to find him.

I didn't make excuses for Anita's choices, but I no longer wanted to punish her for them.

Anita and her family eventually sold the bar and moved from town to a farm in the country. A woman raising kids in the country was a whole lot more acceptable to me than a barmaid. When I left college and moved back to my hometown to marry my high school sweetheart, my husband and I moved into a rental house just down the road from Anita's farm. Soon, we found ourselves spending time at Anita's house. I began to notice qualities in her that I grudgingly admired. She was a good mother to her two adopted children. She liked to cook and sew. She enjoyed gardening and canning, and she liked to make people laugh.

I never would have claimed it growing up, but I was a lot like Anita. We became friends.

I'd drop by Anita's house after work to see the new curtains she'd just made. If it was summer, we would walk out to her garden alongside the barn to see how it was growing. I rummaged through Anita's recipe cards and cookbooks for recipes, copying them to try out on my husband.

I knew our times together made her happy. I also knew she wanted me to accept her as my mother. I wasn't ready.

Like most friendships, ours tended to ebb and flow. After a couple of years, my husband and I left the house down the road from Anita to move to a farm across from my husband's parents. Our sons were born there, and life was busy.

When my own marriage began to falter, I turned to the strongest woman in my life for counsel and solace. My Grandma Mildred, Anita's mother, was the person I trusted most in the world, but Anita and my grandmother had a tenuous relationship, at best. My dependence on Grandma drove a wedge between me and Anita.

My husband and I divorced, and I moved with my two young sons to another town. I seldom saw Anita. Her second family was grown and eventually her second marriage ended in divorce. When I saw her again, Anita had become a different woman. Reclusive, angry, difficult; she insisted she didn't want or need anyone in her life. Our "friendship" was more strained than ever.

There seemed to be no way to relate to who she had become—my birth mother who was no longer even a friend. Other than obligatory visits at Christmas or a card on her birthday, we didn't have much of a relationship. We were back where we had started.

Then the day came when Anita needed me.

Anita's health was failing. I noticed the progression during my intermittent visits to her trailer at the edge of town. She was suffering the effects of mini-strokes and showing signs of dementia. Her adopted daughter lived hours away and her adopted son was "unavailable." My sisters had their own problems. I had remarried and left my career to have two more children. I appeared to be the only one with the time and ability to care for Anita. At her request, I became her caregiver, taking her to doctors' appointments and urging her to take better care of herself. She asked me to be her legal Power of Attorney. I wonder how humbling that must have been for her.

I'm surprised I didn't hesitate when she asked. I held no deep love for this woman, but there was compassion. I could see her pain and sense her loneliness. The feistiness that had carried her through a lifetime of disappointment had drained away. Her self-imposed isolation contributed to her failing health. I think she knew that, because she began calling me and asking me to come and see her.

My visits to Anita's trailer were fraught with regret. Both of us knew we had let the other down. The easiest way for me to respond to her need for affection was through acts of service.

"Can I bring you groceries?"

"Have you taken a walk today? Want to?"

"Are you taking your medicine?

She greeted me with bright smiles, and when I left, she always asked, "When can you come again?"

Anita's health declined quickly and soon she could no longer live alone. She wouldn't accept my hesitant offer to bring her into our home. Instead, she chose to move into a nursing facility on the other side of town.

For Anita, the hardest part of the move was leaving behind the little dog that had been the only bright spot in her lonely life.

Her dog, and the little boy who lived next door.

When she couldn't draw close to her own grandchildren, Anita had opened her heart to this youngster, who visited her a couple of times a week and left his school photos and drawings stuck to her refrigerator door. In a way, it hurt to see evidence of the grandma she hadn't been to my boys. At the same time, it helped to know she had been loved.

Anita gave her much-loved dog to the neighbor boy.

Within a few short months, the woman who once had been sassy, bright and creative, who wrote stories and authored a column for the local newspaper, could barely complete a sentence.

But there were words she needed to say.

"I'm sorry."

Though she'd never once said it in all the years we had navigated our bumpy relationship, she had to say it now. She said it often.

Here I was, fifty-five years old and confused by a woman who had no defined role in my life, accepting her words, along with apologies and gestures that had been a long time coming. I didn't know how to respond.

Head bowed because her body was failing, Anita said other things, in whispers I could barely hear.

"It was best."

"I'm sure you know ..."

"I love you."

I held her hand and told her I understood. Her fingers were limp and cold.

Having spoken the words, she tried telling me not to come to the nursing home. I knew I had to. The forgiveness I had been avoiding for years was beginning to blossom. There were things I needed to tell Anita, too.

Maybe she had made the only choice she could.

Maybe I could forgive her for not being my mother.

Maybe I had learned how to love her.

I continued to visit Anita, usually once a week. I brought food I knew she liked, told her stories about her grandsons, sat with her and watched the Hallmark Channel, wheeled her out into the sunshine or into the dining room. When I told her it was time for me to leave, she no longer told me to stay away. Instead, she asked when I would be back. Perhaps she could see her own stubbornness reflected back at her.

On what I knew would be Anita's last Mother's Day, I thought about all the Mother's Days I had lived with confusion and sadness. The ones when I wanted to deny I had two mothers. The times when I had felt disloyal for sending Anita a card when I loved my stepmom for all she had been to me growing up.

In the years since Anita turned her back and walked down that street, her oldest daughter had learned some things. Life isn't as simple as we'd like. Love is complicated. Sometimes, in our own pain, we make choices that inflict pain on people we love.

Sudden motherhood had been too much for Anita, a girl who barely knew who she was, let alone how to care for three babies. And yet, the young woman who understood all too well what it felt like to be abandoned chose to leave that legacy to her daughters. It took me a long time to come to terms with the abandonment, and it was five decades before I could begin to forgive her for choosing herself over her daughters.

In her final days, seeing herself again as the woman who didn't have the strength to be a mother, Anita wanted me to see it, too. She needed me to understand that walking away was the only thing she felt she had to offer her daughters.

I was with Anita on a sunny afternoon in October when she died. She wasn't aware of what was going on around her, and she couldn't see who was in the room. My stepsister lay curled up next to her in the hospital bed while I sat by her side, holding her hand. It was cold and limp, but I didn't let go.

I wanted to believe Anita knew that this oldest daughter could finally accept a choice she would never fully understand. And that she had chosen to forgive.

Ashes
Ingrid Lochamire

I stood in line for the symbolic smudge of ashes on the first day of Lent, unprepared for what that touch to my forehead would to do my heart.

In the glow of candlelight, tears spilled unbidden. And there she was again, standing at the altar. Skinny, smiling shyly as she posed in her white communion dress, mousy brown hair peeking from beneath a froth of netting, white anklets scrunched above black patent leather shoes. Ardent in her practice of a faith that formed her, the girl's eyes glowed with the joy of taking her first communion. Her first confession.

Her first receiving of the ashes.

Did she know that five decades later she'd stand at another altar and her heart would bust wide open, full with the joy of taking back the precious meaning of the ashes?

I turned away from Catholicism as a high school senior, lured by the popular youth group and upbeat music offered by my friends' non-denominational church. I wanted guitars and games, not incense, chiming bells and Latin liturgy. A copy of The Living Bible went with me to college. My Catholic scriptures were left behind on a bedroom shelf.

An outdoor wedding ceremony officiated by the pastor of that non-denominational church set me on a path toward spiritual awakening and growth. Women in the church mentored and encouraged my still-ardent love for Jesus, and I learned to share Him with others. In years to come, pastors from various denominations and other churches contributed to a deepening faith that sustained me through trials such as divorce, loss, cancer.

The security of a faith built on decades spent living out God's Word among His people allowed me to listen when a gentle ripple of longing began to surface. In the beginning, I couldn't put a word to the yearnings that bubbled in a quiet corner of my soul. I love my church. I'm in deep agreement with the doctrine and theology of our evangelical protestant beliefs and practices. But, like a lamp lit by a low-wattage bulb, my rock-solid faith lacked some of the glow that burned across the years from the altar of that little Catholic chapel of my childhood.

Then last summer I met two faithful women doing a work of revival at a Catholic retreat center, and the yearnings slipped into place.

Beauty, symbolism, tradition, corporate prayer, holy seasons. I had shed them like an ill-fitting coat in my youth. Now, I felt the loss of their weight and warmth.

I soaked up the joy of those women doing a work for Jesus, offering to add a work of my own to their revival project. As we talked and planned, I recognized and understood what shone from their eyes when they spoke to me of tradition. Of miracles, healings, sacraments. Of a church history that, in many ways, all Christian faiths share.

It was familiar because it was part of me.

My stepmom passed away shortly after these women completed their project. It was inevitable that my grieving was bound up by their unwavering commitment to the Church. And by my stepmother's. Her collection of Catholic icons, prayer books, rosaries, holy medals and other symbols of faith passed through my hands. They gave weight once again to what I'd known and lived, to the faith that formed me.

You can turn from one good thing and replace it with another. But can you wipe away the imprint that one thing left on your soul? Or can you acknowledge the stirrings and make space for them to be welcomed in the now?

Our evangelical Christian church chose to observe Ash Wednesday for the first time in many years. Dipping back into the dust of a tradition that lay at the foundation of my faith brought me face to face with the ardent little Catholic girl who was the Bride of Jesus.

Her eyes still glow.

> "Remember, man, that thou art dust and unto dust thou shalt return." Genesis 3:19b

A Walk Among the Tombstones
Ingrid Lochamire

It was not what I expected to do on an Easter Sunday evening.

We had worshiped, feasted and rested. Our hearts and bellies were full with the celebration of Christ's resurrection. Who knew as the sun was setting we'd be walking among the dead and rejoicing over life?

An evening visit to my hometown on Easter Sunday led us to Rose Hill Cemetery. Dad spent several years as keeper of the cemetery grounds and records. It was his very favorite job among the many he'd held in his eighty-five years, and he knew the layout of this beautiful resting place like the back of his hand. (He did, in fact, survey and map out a portion of the cemetery. He also gave walking tours as part of the Tombstone Trail, an organized trek through ten cemeteries in northeast Indiana.)

On this beautiful spring evening, we were there to see the stone bench he and Mom had placed on the site where they would be buried. It was a lovely black marble piece of art that was engraved with icons depicting their character and interests. A drawing of the Virgin Mary with a coiled rosary reflected Mom's deep Catholic roots. Dad's military service was honored with a sketch of the B-52 bomber that carried him in its belly for tours across the United States during his peacetime enlistment.

We inspected the beautiful piece and listened to Dad explain that the bomber's wings were a little short. He half-jokingly mentioned bringing a dremel tool to the cemetery to correct the problem. Ever the fixer-upper.

Venturing into the older parts of the rolling burial grounds, we found stones bearing the names of my great-grandparents and other individuals who contributed to my hometown's history. As we walked and drove the winding pathways, familiar names passed before us. Prickett, Moorhouse, Black, Brazzell, Young—families whose lives were entwined with mine during my growing-up years in this small town.

Far off, the Lutheran Church downtown chimed the hour, and suddenly I was transported back to summer evenings spent playing among the tombstones.

One particular summer—perhaps the BEST summer of my youth, because that's what memories do for us—a group of my school friends organized "kick-the-can" contests on side streets downtown. This crazy game of hide-and-seek that we played with great passion helped fill our summer evenings and sometimes led us to the cemetery where the tombstones made perfect hiding spots.

A few years later, some high school chums had the great idea to make a late-night visit to the cemetery, maybe to relive our youth or maybe just because it was something to do.

We loaded ourselves into a couple of cars and drove across town to the cemetery gate. The stone markers propped against the night sky had a chilling effect. We parked the car behind some trees and, hearts racing, scrambled across the cemetery for a commemorative game of hide-and-seek. Exuberant in our innocence (drugs and alcohol were not part of our social lives, at least not openly), our voices rang out into the night and carried across the road to my uncle's house.

Uncle Joe was my "cool" uncle. A handsome former high school basketball star, he was my favorite uncle. But he now had a wife and a young family, and they were the unofficial guardians of Rose Hill Cemetery.

Soon, headlights appeared at the entrance to the cemetery. Uncle Joe had called the town cops. We were busted.

A few brave souls took off, but I promptly and obediently came out from behind the tombstone hiding spot in response to the policeman's call. He gathered those he could find and hauled us to the police station where our names were written down and our parents were called. I realize now that he had to be fighting back a chuckle as he took in our fear-struck faces and contrite countenance.

On an Easter Sunday evening, back among the tombstones, it was somehow comforting to walk among the dead and to recall moments that speak to me of life.

"Assisted Living"
Ingrid Lochamire

I want to laugh, but there's no punchline. Instead, tears flow salty with sorrow.

Ten years past—even two—his saucy words would have given me a chuckle. Not today.

A sailor's tongue, unleashed by frustration, spews profanity in my face. Nothing careless or casual in that phrase. No habitual harangue there. Just honest words that slice and slap. They carve his pain into my flesh.

Yet, he feels it more than me. He's carried it longer and deeper. A father's trust and a love without bounds sour in his spittle before the words leaves his lips.

"Shot to hell."

"Damn it all."

"What the fuck am I doing here?"

Whispered in defeat, they scream injustice, foul play, unfair. Life sucks.

"Is this all there is?" he moans.

Yes, Dad. It is.

Eighty-eight years wind down to this: a narrow bed, a lone recliner, food you despise, people you don't know feeding you pills without labels. No home. No work. No car. No wife. Stripped of purpose and pride. Naked, with nothing to hide.

Is this all there is? He gave me the world, and I give him this? He deserves more than "assisted living."

"I pray to God none of my family ever has to live like this. It ain't living."

No, it ain't.

He turns back to me, spent and repentant. Bony shoulders lift a sigh.

"Could be worse," he says. We don't believe it but pretend it's true.

Anger wears on thin places; defeat moves in. The recliner beckons. A wave of the TV remote signals dismissal. I turn quickly so he won't see my tears, though I'm sure he's not looking.

I, too, am spent, repentant.

I love you, Dad.

"Yeah. I know ..."

Stones
Ingrid Lochamire

I grew up in a little stone house at the edge of a small midwestern town. Years before we moved there, a previous owner had covered his simple, wood-frame house with big rocks of all shapes and sizes. Set together with mortar, like bricks, the stones transformed a plain square structure into a unique, fanciful cottage with curved archways and an attached grape arbor. Growing up in that stone house fueled my childhood daydreams and offered the perfect setting for a little girl's vivid imagination.

On warm summer afternoons, my sisters and I often wandered around the perimeter of our stone house, looking at the different rocks, trying to guess where they might have been found. For the longest time, I thought the builder must have hauled them there from exotic sites around the world. I was disappointed to learn later that most were found in the fields in and around my hometown.

During one of those summers, I embarked on a quest to read through our set of Encyclopedia Britannica. I spent a good amount of time looking up the names of the rocks, and when my "R" volume of the encyclopedia didn't yield enough information, I tracked down a guide to rocks and minerals at the library. Searching out the names and descriptions of the rocks that I lived under occupied me for days.

Of course, I soon lost interest and never did complete my research, but I also never tired of running my hands over those stones. Rough, sharply jagged, smooth and glossy, porous or striped.

Mingled in with the glistening blacks and speckled browns and smooth grays were quite a few dull white slabs of Indiana limestone. Though lacking in beauty and with a less-than-exotic name and origin, limestone is one of the strongest of natural building materials. Entire buildings are constructed of limestone and have been standing for centuries. The oldest and largest of the Great Egyptian Pyramids was built of limestone block over 4,000 years ago.

To the east of those pyramids, across the Red Sea and a couple thousand years later, Christ the "living stone" built his earthly church on a "piece of rock"—petros. Peter.

Peter the Rock called Christ "the living stone—rejected by humans but chosen by God and precious to him." But then he turned around and reminded us in his writings that, as co-heirs with Christ, we "like living stones, are being built into a spiritual house to be a holy priesthood."

Living stones, gathered together, piled high, built up to become a dwelling place for the Holy Spirit, designed to represent Christ the King as a "holy priesthood."

Quite an honor for simple stones.

My childhood home still stands, strong and solid, at the end of Fourth Street. A different family is creating memories within those behind stone-clad walls. I hope they are happy memories.

Unlike stones fashioned into an earthly dwelling, we, as "living" stones, are gathered together, piled high, built up to testify to the One who dwells within. Upon our doorpost is written the name of *Christ the Priest, the Original Living Stone*. We stand—a holy priesthood— to point others to "the stone the builders rejected" who "has become the cornerstone" (Psalm 118:22).

An Unexpected Journey
Ingrid Lochamire

Life is a journey, but I believe God walks with us through the valleys and onto the mountaintops, through our joys and our trials. I have walked near Jesus and at times I've turned down my own path. But "He who searches the hearts" (Rom. 8:27) never turned from me. I've never felt God's presence more than when I walked through a season with breast cancer.

I was scheduled for a mammogram in December 2012, right after Christmas. More tests over the next two weeks revealed that I had a small cancerous tumor that was growing quickly. The New Year was ushered in with more tests, surgery and radiation. I was fortunate that the cancer was found early, and my recovery was swift. Today I am cancer-free.

The word "cancer" stops even the strongest of us in our tracks. I felt so vulnerable, yet at the same time so safe. God provided a peace that sustained me through this season. During the weeks following the diagnosis, I shared some of my thoughts and prayers regarding this new reality in life's landscape. Perhaps these reflections will ease the journey for others dealing with cancer.

The Answer to Anxiety
January 14, 2013

Today I must admit to being anxious. In the six days since I learned I have a cancerous tumor growing in my left breast, I have given myself just five minutes to cry and grieve over what might come of this. Behind a closed door, I questioned and wept, but then I walked out onto the path laid out before me. Conversations with doctors, with family and with dear friends fed the peace I pursued so doggedly, just as the estrogen is feeding my one-centimeter tumor. And I've walked in that peace, saying what I believe: that God knows, that He's known from the womb, that He cares and that He wastes nothing.

Good *will* come from this ... even this.

But today I am anxious. In two hours I will get in my car and travel to the hospital, where I'll don that blue cape that opens in the front, and I'll do exactly what they tell me, walk where they lead for tests in preparation for the surgeon's knife. I'll pray as I walk and wait, as others are praying for me, for a good outcome, for a simple, straight-forward removal of the cancer. For those words of comfort—"We got it all. That's it. You can get on with your life."

So today, as I'm anxious, and as only God could ordain, my devotional tells me this:

"The answer to anxiety is the adoration of Christ."[1]

Author Ann Voskamp quotes John Calvin and I am reminded that even in this, I can rejoice, I can adore, I can exalt Christ. I can *thank* Him for this trial, for the fear that has pulled me closer to Him and to those I love.

On this of surgery, I trust God for a right outcome, I really do. His "right" may not be mine, but I pledge to exalt Him in it, to give Him the glory for healing, for the wisdom of doctors, for the faith of family and friends.

I can't do much heavy lifting immediately after this surgery, but I can do a little dancing, a little lifting of hands in worship and praise. Were I a braver soul, I could be dancing down the hallways of the hospital in my silly blue cape, exalting and

---

1 Ann Voskamp. "One Thousand Gifts." Zondervan, 2011

adoring Him who created me and has known me from the womb ... knows me even now.

At the very least, I can say, "Thank you, God, for even this."

Body on Loan from God
January 18, 2013

In the days since a cancerous tumor was lifted from my chest, I've thought a lot about this earthly body, the one God created for me over sixty years ago. These days, I am certainly aware that my body and I are on the downhill side of life.

If I'm lucky (or maybe not), I could spend another twenty years in this sack of bones, muscle and skin. No doubt this recent encounter with exploding cancer cells will not be my last health issue, nor was it my first. As a friend and I joked recently, we've all been dying since the day we were born.

It helps to remember that this body, this "temple" of heavenly design, is not my eternal vessel. It is a disposable wrapper, serving a purpose and giving a visible image to the soul God set inside when He first knew me in my mother's womb. To borrow a notion from my husband's favorite conservative radio personality, I have a body "on loan from God."*

A wise little girl awakened in me thoughts about our heavenly bodies years ago when she described the day she would be able to walk into Jesus' arms. This little one, now a grown woman, hasn't been able to walk or stand unassisted for more than a few seconds since birth. A neurological defect took that ability from her, but in its place, God set a sweet spirit and blazing faith that have carried her more miles than I'll ever walk. Brown eyes snapping, little Gertie told her mother's friends that she couldn't wait until she gets her new body in heaven so she can run with the other children ... and stand beside Jesus.

Yesterday, a dear friend who is walking his own journey with cancer asked me how I'm seeing life these days. "How has your perspective changed?" he said. I know that his has. A beloved husband, father to six and "Papa" to four grandchildren, he knows what he will leave behind should cancer take him from his earthly home. I've seen him cherishing each day with his family. And I've watched him grow closer to his Lord and Savior.

This friend pointed me to words of another who has tasted the word "cancer" on the tongue, and who is anointed by God to speak hard truths full of the Holy Spirit. In his book *Don't Waste Your Cancer*, author and pastor John Piper says this:

"We will waste our cancer if we don't hear in our own groanings the labor pains of the new creation." Piper points out that "glorious freedom is coming"—freedom from sin, from pain, from these earthly bodies that will fail us.

"Don't misinterpret your own groanings. Don't waste the witness of your own cancer," says Piper. "The aim of God in our cancer (among a thousand other good things) is to knock props out from under our hearts so that we rely utterly on him."

So, I'm reminded that God doesn't waste anything, that this cancer is part of His plan for me, and that He will use it for good … is using it even now. Today, that good is to draw me deeper into His Word, to cause me to lean into Him for strength, to turn toward those who love me enough to walk alongside in this journey. And to set my eyes on the day I can stand perfect and whole beside my heavenly Father.

I got the answer I prayed for yesterday—the tumor is gone and no cancer cells were left behind. I will be writing my own answer to a bigger question in the days to come: How will I choose to spend the days I have left walking on this earth? If I take John

Piper's advice, I'll choose not to waste this thing that God has allowed in my life.

"For this light momentary affliction is preparing for us an eternal weight of glory beyond all comparison" 2 Corinthians 4:17

I'm counting on that "glory beyond all comparison."

*Thank you, Rush Limbaugh

No "Muskrat Love" in My World
January 26, 2013

Taking stock recently of my body's collision with breast cancer, I'm intrigued by how God has tucked so many life lessons into this natural world, almost as if He's devised a sort of "treasure hunt" for us. It was with amusement that I stumbled upon a lesson in "Muskrat Love" buried for me in my own back yard.

One has taken up residence in our pond; a muskrat, that is. I first spied him just after Christmas, before the ice, and while winter delayed its coming. Walking the pond's sunlit edge, I heard a splash. A long, flat tail slithered behind a lump of fur below the glassy surface. I stood still, quiet, waiting, when a pointy nose pierced the surface, followed by beady eyes. A rippled wake marked the muskrat's progress across the spring-fed pond. Just as suddenly, he was gone and the water calmed.

Since that first sighting, I've been able to watch him from my kitchen window or from a second-story bathroom. Some days, I miss his travels across the pond. The surface remains unbroken, no wake appears. Other days, I spy his slick head or catch sight of the ripples his journey creates. I know from my husband, who trapped wildlife as a boy, that the muskrat is probably burrowing into the walls of the pond we dredged in the fall. No doubt he's creating a home for the family he hopes to breed come spring.

On these deep winter days, as I walk the edge of this pool of uncertainty and concern, I remind myself that I have owned the fact "cancer" is now part of my personal vocabulary, and there is acceptance of what must be done and what may come. I trust God "has this" and I'm leaning into Him for comfort, and into the love of those who surround me. Most days, there is calm, peace.

But then there are days when a churning begins beneath the surface and I sense some burrowing deep in the strong wall of faith I've built. A doubt, a tremble of fear, an essence of frustration—they break the surface and I dwell in them a bit. It feels good to vent a little, to stir the waters and examine what lies beneath. But before long, I see that they threaten to displace this peace I've worked to attain. And as I watch the ripples wash over my family, spill into my daily duties, I realize that if I don't grab these feelings by the tail, they will set up housekeeping in my world, ready to burrow in and build a room for breeding.

My husband says the muskrat must go. Where, I wonder? How? But I know too well the plans he has for it, and I protest. Muskrats need a place to live, too, I say. Not here, he says. Where there's one, there will soon be others, and they'll wreck the foundation we worked to create in the depths of this peaceful pond.

I have to agree. There is no room for them—*for muskrats or doubts, frustrations or fears*—not here, not in our world.

Reflecting on Lessons Learned
February 2, 2013

Lying on a gurney in the radiation room at my cancer treatment center, I count up to sixteen.

"You're number sixteen," I say to the kind fellow prepping me for my morning CAT scan. Number sixteen in a long line of strangers to examine, poke, bandage or photograph this rather personal area of my body. He chuckles and pushes a button that slides me into the scanning tunnel. All in a day's work.

Some journeys we plan, others are mapped out for us, and still others we just stumble upon. I certainly didn't plan my journey through breast cancer, though I believe God knew all along that it would become part of His plan for me. I stumbled upon it through a routine mammogram. And now, it seems a new course is mapped out for me.

The ten radiation treatments I received over the past week were not on my original calendar for January 2013, but the appointments scribbled in the pages of my Day-Timer and on the refrigerator calendar represent signposts on this journey. And the diploma and mug I received from the hospital staff on the day of my last radiation treatment tell me I've turned a corner with some new life lessons under my belt.

Here's what I've learned so far at this intersection with breast cancer:

- **Expect the unexpected.** At sixty (and as the mom of four sons), you'd think I'd have learned that one by now, but cynicism has never been part of my makeup. I tend to live on the sunny side of life, which means I occasionally get blindsided by reality. In this reality, I'm finding unexpected blessings— God speaking to me in nature, friendships that grow deeper through this shared experience, the pleasure of a warm blanket wrapped around my shoulders by a stranger doing her job with kindness.
- **Lean on those who have traveled this path before you.** I have never met author and pastor John Piper, but his thoughtful writings on the eve of his surgery for prostate cancer are like advice from a godly friend. In *Don't Waste Your Cancer*, Piper reminds all of us walking through trial that illness or troubles of any kind are not a "curse." Our lives have been "transformed from a punitive pathway to hell into a purifying pathway to heaven. We are not cursed.

As hard as it is to feel this, we believe God is not withholding good. He is doing good."*

The Lord God is a sun and shield; the Lord bestows favor and honor. No good thing does he withhold from those who walk uprightly.
(Psalm 84:11)

- **It's not enough to just have a "positive attitude."** We need to walk the talk. In her book *There's No Place Like Hope*, cancer survivor Vickie Girard said, "You can't just sit around and visualize your way to wellness with positive thoughts. I think it's important that we connect our positive attitude to forward-moving action or activity." Like The Little Engine That Could, we can say "I think I can, I think I can," but then we've got to build up the steam to make it up that hill. For me, that means learning all I can about this chronic disease, building good nutrients into my diet, taking the right medication and making myself exercise every day. That last one will be the toughest, unless I reward it with dark, dark chocolate (Yes, that's in my new diet).
- **It's okay to put yourself first once in a while.** I can be self-sacrificial to a fault. I'm realizing the good feeling I get from putting others first is really self-serving if in doing that I risk becoming a burden myself. We do for others if we do not do for ourselves. Whatever it is that we need for rejuvenation should be built into our days. And we shouldn't ruin it by feeling guilty. Taking time for "self" is one of the best things we can do for those who share our days.
- **Appreciate the world God has given to us.** Today is a time to *appreciate* the people, places and events that are woven into my life.

- **A sense of humor helps.** (See the Number Sixteen observation above.) I intend to laugh a lot more in the days ahead.

I'm sure there's much more to be learned in this experience and in life. These lessons are a good start—or maybe they should be called a "restart," because as long as we're breathing, we should be learning.

"Don't Waste Your Cancer," an essay by John Piper, Desire God (2006)
There's No Place Like Hope, Vickie Girard, Compendium Publishing & Communications (2008)

Author Biographies

DeVonna R. Allison is a freelance writer and Marine Corps veteran whose work has been featured in *Country Woman* magazine, *Horse and Rider* magazine, *Purpose* magazine, *the Upper Room*, *Mennonite World Review*, the *Secret Place* magazine, *Proud to Be*, volume three, *Chicken Soup for the Soul: Miracles Happen*, and *The Binnacle: Literary Magazine of Coastal Maine*. DeVonna and her husband make their home in southern Michigan, where they live in a house in the woods with their two bulldogs.

Monica Clark works with children and moonlights at a hardware store. She is the proud mother of a thoughtful son, a delightful daughter-in-law and a talented fifteen-year-old. She lives in northern Indiana with her husband, daughter and an absurdly indifferent cat. Her stories and poems have been published in *Highlights for Children*, *Balloons Lit Journal*, *Alfred Hitchcock's Mystery Magazine* and several poetry anthologies. She is also the recipient of the Dana Literary Award for poetry.

Shanda Blue Easterday's poems have been published in the *The Dos Passos Review*, *Dislocate*, *The Louisville Review*, *The Southern Indiana Review*, *Suspension*, and *Flying Island*. Her poetry collection *The Beekeeper's Wife* was published in 2011 and a chapbook *From Egg to Moth*, poems about Maria Sybilla Marian, as well. She is a retired professor of Literatures in English, and editor for Mind Vine Press.

Hedy Habra has authored two poetry collections, *Under Brushstrokes*, finalist for the USA Best Book Award and the

International Poetry Book Award, and *Tea in Heliopolis*, winner of the USA Best Book Award and finalist for the International Poetry Book Award. Her story collection, *Flying Carpets*, won the Arab American National Book Award's Honorable Mention and was finalist for the Eric Hoffer Award. A recipient of the Nazim Hikmet Poetry Award, she was a six-time nominee for the Pushcart Prize and Best of the Net. Her work appears in *Cimarron Review*, *The Bitter Oleander*, *Blue Fifth Review*, *Cider Press Review*, *Drunken Boat*, *Gargoyle*, *Nimrod*, *Poet Lore*, *World Literature Today* and *Verse Daily*. Her website is hedyhabra.com

Ingrid Lochamire is a former news reporter and award-winning feature writer for a regional news outlet. She "retired" from journalism to homeschool her four sons, now all graduated. Ingrid and her husband live in a 140-year-old farm house in northeast Indiana, where she shares her own "slice of life" experiences and reflections on her blog and elsewhere. She also encourages others to capture and tell their life stories and has created a tool to help them do so. Ingrid's work has appeared on various websites and in the literary journal *Topology*. She is a member of Redbud Writers Guild and her essays have been featured in *The Redbud Post*. She self-published the book *One Man's Work*, stories from her father's life.

Kathleen McGookey's work has appeared in journals including *Crazyhorse*, *Denver Quarterly*, *Epoch*, *Field*, *Indiana Review*, *Ploughshares*, *The Prose Poem: An International Journal*, *Prairie Schooner*, *Quarterly West*, *Rhino*, *Seneca Review*, and *West Branch*. Her book *Heart in a Jar* was published by White Pine Press in Spring 2017. She has also published two other books of poems, two chapbooks and a book of translations of French poet Georges Godeau's prose poems.

Adela Najarro is the author of three poetry collections: *Split Geography*, *Twice Told Over* and *My Childrens*, a chapbook that includes teaching resources. With *My Childrens* she hopes to bring Latinx poetry into the classroom so that students can explore poetry, identity and what it means to be Latinx in US society. Each poem in the collection is accompanied by a nonfiction comment, a writing prompt, comprehension questions, and "Look It Up!" suggestions. She teaches creative writing, literature, and composition at Cabrillo College. More information about Adela can be found at her website: www.adelanajarro.com.

Traci Rhoades writes from her kitchen table in rural Michigan, not far at all from Lake Michigan's shoreline. When she first started blogging at tracesoffaith.com, she wondered about what unique voice she could bring. She's landed on this one-line description: A Country Girl Goes to Church.

Patricia Jabbeh Wesley is a Liberian civil war survivor who immigrated to the United States with her family during the Liberian civil war. She is the author of five books of poetry: *When the Wanderers Come Home*, *Where the Road Turns*, *The River is Rising*, *Becoming Ebony* and *Before the Palm Could Bloom: Poems of Africa*. She is also the author of a children's book, *In Monrovia, the River Visits the Sea*. Her poem "One Day: Love Song for Divorced Women" was selected by US Poet Laureate Ted Kooser for *American Life in Poetry*. Her work has been anthologized and published around the world. She teaches at Penn State Altoona.

Art Credits

Cover Design Ingrid Lochamire, "Sunflowers" painting by Cheryl DenBoer

Genre Dividers designed by Ingrid Lochamire, "Lemons" painting by Matt Kalasky,

"Red Onions" painting by Pat Asbury, "Strawberries" painting by Preston,

"Amaryllis" painting by Vivian Schilling, "Teapot" painting by Darlene Mowatt.

Blue Shutters, Green Door, Apartment Building, "51" photographs in France by Martha Faketty

Barn, Birds' Nest, Creek, Crucifix, Grass and Sun, Hammock and Ash Cross photographs by Ingrid Lochamire

Wall photograph by DeVonna Allison